Without A Voice

Without A Voice

One Woman's Fight For Justice

Michelle Nicholson

First published in 2017

Copyright © Michelle Nicholson 2017

The right of Michelle Nicholson to be identified as the Author of the Work.

A CIP catalogue record for this title is available from the British Library.

ISBN

978-1-9997038-0-6

Based on a true story

Disclaimer

I have tried to recreate events, locales and conversations from my memories of
them. In order to maintain their anonymity, in some instances I have changed the
names of individuals and may have changed some identifying characteristics.

Dedicated To

The Unheard

In Loving Memory Of

My gentle, loving and protective father,
who taught me true values and morals in humanity.
Keith Arthur Nicholson
6 June 1946 ~ 9 September 1993

Acknowledgements

For my daughter – an inspirational woman and a loving mother.

I thank my mother for doing her best whilst suffering from a severe mental health disposition – I have outlined my memories of her in this book to illustrate how my character was built – despite her disability she continues to try her best.

A very special thank you to Mickey and Jo who have been unfailingly loyal and supportive in their belief of my innocence.

Thank you to all those who helped me resettle.

To all those who support me at *Key Changes – Unlocking Women's Potential*, a charity I founded after my release from prison in 2012, I deeply thank you for your support to continue helping women in the criminal justice system.

If, after reading this book, anyone is willing to offer any legal expertise or investigation to support my efforts to clear my name, please make contact through my website.

Prologue - The Prophecy

I found myself standing at the bottom of the stairs again. They were so familiar by now, as it had become a regular journey I took by night. Nothing ever changed; the event remained the same, every time, right down to the fine detail. It was cold, bleak and dark. A gripping sense of horror engulfed me to the point where I thought it could take away my breath. The feeling was so intense, I felt it might even take my young life. Looking up to the top of the stairs, I knew I had no option but to climb them, but why? Why? I knew, too, that I had to climb to the very top, where the light shone through the crack under the bottom of the door, its glow making the gloomy staircase somehow more threatening.

As I was imagining that journey, I noticed again the person standing by my side; who was it? With my attention riveted on the staircase, the person seemed almost irrelevant; all I knew was that the stranger would ensure I reached the top, with or without my will.

I dragged my attention to the stranger.

"Why do I have to go?" I asked, breaking the silence, uncomfortably, to the comforter or the captor; it was hard for me to tell the difference.

I was pleading, I knew it; I could hear it in the pitch of my voice. There was no mistaking that I would beg if I thought it would make even a slight bit of difference in stopping the journey to the top of those stairs.

I knew when I spoke the words they were useless; the silent woman looked sombrely at me, as if she was leading me to my death. *Why didn't she help me?*

There was no mistaking the fear building inside of me, led by the staircase itself and in its darkness, I began to climb, holding on to the banisters as if they could save me. With each step, the fear deepened. Half way up, a short landing, about a metre in length, gave me the reason I desperately needed to pause the journey.

I pleaded again, "Why do I have to go?"

I had never, in my short life, felt so much fear as I did taking this terrible journey night after night. There was another emotion, something I had not experienced and could not articulate, but it horrified me, magnifying a nightmare I could not describe. It was so powerful I feared, again, it might kill me. My plea fell on deaf ears and as I started to climb the staircase once more, the fear escalated to a terrifying new dimension.

That's when I screamed. I didn't know I was screaming. Not in this nightmare world, but in another world, my screams were heard. That was when the four-year-old me would wake again, with the same familiar person by my side, my comforter.

"It's OK, you're safe, Michelle." His words were kind, his voice was warm, and I was safe. I stopped screaming as I became aware of my surroundings, as if I had been suddenly transported from one world to another. It had seemed so real.

My father looked concerned. I loved him; he was warm.

"It's OK," he repeated calmly, as I became fully aware of his presence.

He was an expert at reassurance; my father was here, without fail, by my side. I loved him and there was no doubt that he loved me.

He would often ask me, "Tell me about your dream Michelle?"

Even at my young age, I knew it troubled him. My mind searched for reasoning and words to explain it to him; my child's mind also somehow knew I couldn't make him understand the power of the emotions which made me cry out. I didn't have the vocabulary or the experience to explain them as I do now. It was obvious my father was trying to solve some kind of riddle, to unlock my mind. He seemed concerned, even desperate, to do so.

"Tell me again," he would often say, looking like he was fitting together a puzzle that he *had* to solve.

He would wipe the perspiration from my forehead until I felt safe enough to close my eyes. His kindness and concern would always make me feel safe enough to sleep again. Just looking into those eyes, his kind and gentle warm soul, I was able to absorb into the very centre of the unconditional love he held for me. I felt safe and loved.

How ironic that eighteen years later, this dream or nightmare became my only comforter. It has become the only answer to many unresolved questions in my life; questions that I know are the source of equally many, perhaps even more nightmares.

The world I live in now has changed and I live my life in the nightmare and the dream. Oh yes, the dream, has become my only comforter and I often cling onto its strength in reassurance of its symbol of destiny. The dream, which recurred for ten years of my young life, showed a glimpse of what was to come. Which was the dream and which was the nightmare?

The dream was the awakening from the nightmare, the gentle comforting reassurance as I transitioned the two worlds of differing realities. The nightmare is knowing that one of them would become an actual, lived, horrifying reality in both worlds and that there was no awakening from it into a place of comfort or safety.

The staircase, so recurrent in those early years, turned out to be the staircase to the Crown Court in Sheffield. The feelings from those childhood nocturnal terrors mirrored exactly the intense shock of being found guilty of a crime which I was helpless to stop. The reluctance of those same past experiences was an exact replica of the later surreal absurdity of being made to stand next to a man who had committed that crime, as if I had been the main cause of his behaviour; a man who had been promised that, by giving evidence against me, he would receive a lesser sentence for himself.

The horror which awaited me at the top of those stairs – the horror of the guilty verdict – did almost kill me, as the shock slammed through my body.

The dream, however, for me now, suggests that our lives have been already mapped out and even though we make choices, they always lead to what is mapped out; our destiny. Nothing I could have ever done would have prevented the nightmare from beginning. This is my only comfort as I try to repave the past. Only now, my father is not there to comfort me. Nobody is. I am alone and lost.

Introduction

Have you ever looked back on your life with a philosophical mind, and thought deeply about how and why your mindset came to be, at certain, and sometimes critical times?

Understanding the evolving mind in its environment, and not as an isolated process, is something that's easier for an individual who has experienced a specific time and event. It is harder for those who have not had that experience to comprehend, even though they may be told the story over and over.

The fact is that even though we are an intelligent species, the human mind is underestimated in its decision making power. The human mind is able to incapacitate you, causing you not to act at a critical moment, or it can make you believe you can climb the highest mountain in the world.

The concept of mind over matter, I believe, is simply true. By thinking and overcoming our own obstacles, we place in our mind strong beliefs that can overcome many wider physical and societal oppressions and constraints. It's not so easy, however, to understand how your original thought processes came into place in any given moment. Clarity comes as life evolves and you start to experience different social situations in which new comparisons can be made, and then clearer understandings emerge, as you become the outsider looking in to your own life.

That's exactly where I am now, an outsider looking in, telling a story as truthfully as I can, with the perceptions and experiences as they were, and have evolved – without prejudice – with a deep understanding of a whole array of circumstances. No longer seeing the world in black and white, or right or wrong, my story is told without the harsh and unforgiving process by which our communities are often encouraged and shaped to become.

As a young girl, I always remembered wanting more from life than I saw around me at the time. I didn't want to accept the standards of my environment, which meant that life for a young woman was having children at a young age. Looking out of the window one day, deep in thought, I realised, if I were to stay where I am, there's a big possibility that I may end up as a woman with no opportunities, with three or four children, like so many of the middle aged women in our community struggling to make ends meet.

I looked around my environment and ventured to step a rung up the community ladder, by being the first in my family to gain qualifications and a respectable job, like the jobs I knew so many others parents at school did. The rung was there, but it lacked support. Life for many around me appeared to be doomed from the start.

It's often hard for me to understand how vulnerable I was as a young woman. I try to be compassionate towards her, my younger self, as I accept all her mistakes and the situations she found herself in as a result of her naivety. I was often in search of love and happiness, not understanding that all those things are found within and not around you.

I was easy prey to many and life to that point had rendered me incapable of speaking out and making decisions for myself. I wanted to be able to speak my mind, and to make good, strong, positive decisions for myself. But it was as if my voice had been stunted from growing up with constant criticism, which programmed my mind to send a message to myself that whatever I was about to say, or the decision I was about to make, was stupid, in the millisecond before that decision or voice was about to emerge. It prevented my voice from being heard or acted upon and it incapacitated me.

I looked to others for their decisions and their voice, because mine was oppressed by my own thinking and programming, almost as if I had no voice of my own. My mother's voice over the years of growing up had turned into my own thinking, telling me I was worthless or that my decisions were stupid. I looked to others for approval before I spoke. I strove to figure out what others were thinking, even as I criticised my own thoughts, just as my mother had done. I had no way of knowing how to be myself. A large part of me didn't even know who I truly was, and the other part of me bombarded my consciousness with criticisms and put-downs.

Yet I still kept a goal to find someone to love me, to make me happy, to escape from the loneliness which had marred my childhood. It was a lonely childhood, without love from a mother who'd rejected me very early on. A child whose mother was lonely and ill herself, suffering from the mental illness of schizophrenia, a mother whose outward aggression and hatred focused intensely on the only person around her, her daughter, me.

Growing up in such an environment developed into withdrawal and isolation for me, even though I lived with my mother. My childhood was one without positive communication and love, only constant criticism.

The social circumstances of growing up on a small council estate also shaped my thinking; I underestimated, or was simply unaware of, the level of poverty in the local area. From an early age, I realised that as young boys, my brother and his circle of friends on the estate had become involved in crime. I recall the shame and disappointment in the family, from my father and my mother. I experienced the *hush*; we were not allowed to talk about visiting him in the detention centre.

All I understood was that my brother might be lonely and in need of comfort. But I wasn't allowed to see him in that place and therefore began thinking that my part of the local community was wrong and the authorities were right.

An attempt to be like everyone else was my thinking – everyone else, that is, who was not part of what I perceived as the particular section of the community in which I found myself. To attempt to fit into the norms set by the wider and apparently more acceptable society and not to stand out as being different. I was already acutely aware that people treated my family and me differently. I wondered why they treated us so differently and why they used their tone and distance in a manner that was noticeable even to a child.

I longed not to hear those tones, or feel that distance, even if that meant trying to fit into the norm, but I wasn't sure what that norm was. I looked up to authority figures, relying on them for the truth. After all, they set the social standards of right and wrong, and those standards had clear consequences for those who didn't meet them – the starkest consequence being exclusion in its many forms.

As I saw it, the authorities were abiding by their own set of standards and leading by example for the disadvantaged and poor, people like us – the class of people who struggled to find meaningful work and opportunities – the *criminals*. I watched my brother's friend take what he thought was owed to him to have a better life – he was a young man who rebelled against that system and it seemed the only way for him to escape it. In that era, none of my community had an opportunity to be educated at university that may result in securing professional and meaningful work.

My grandfather had worked in a factory all his life and died only a couple of years after his retirement. He was a hard-working man and left the world illustrating the outcome of a hard-working man in a deprived area. He had never gone abroad or bought a car, they were only dreams in our community. He worked to live and was never able to afford a mortgage, so he remained on the council backstreets his entire life.

Our street represented people working with meaningless tasks or not working at all, as an opt-out of their limited choices. We were separated from others in the town who had opportunities, who easily bought cars and held professional jobs. They appeared to have more meaningful lives than us. I felt a lesser human being to the norm because of the divide and this stereotype was reiterated by my critic, my mother.

I've learnt over the years that many apparent societal values are held to be less important than the way you appear. Take my father's long hair and his worn clothes. Did this mean that he was less of a person than a businessman wearing a suit, even though he has individual values such as integrity, truth and wisdom? He would be given strange looks walking down the street and I noticed he was glared at in shops. To be respected for the size of your heart and the respect you give to other people seems less important than the street you grow up in; what you look like; what clothes you wear; where you are in the societal ladder from the unemployed to the elite and powerful.

I came to realise that many people in authorities have been exposed for their corrupt behaviours and horrific abuses of authority have come to light, affecting innocent members of the society and the community. The helpless, the poor, the deprived and communities like mine.

Yet there are many I have met, from those very communities, who have huge hearts and whom I will never forget. The first person I encountered in this very special group was my father. He had a big heart and struggled with the unjust standards set by society. He was a loving, honest man; all of the traits he held were important and valuable aspects of true humanity.

Many young women in prison are the victims of horrific and heinous crimes before they become the perpetrators of several more minor crimes. I learnt that more often than not, women serving sentences had suffered from sexual, physical and or mental abuse. Had they had justice, their perpetrators would have served long sentences, but many of them blame themselves, reflecting the standards set by society. They know they have done wrong and at the same time, most of them blame themselves for the abuse. Most of them say, "*I was a difficult child; I deserved it.*"

They have given up on themselves before society has and this is the main reason why they reoffend; they cannot find a way to fit into society any more. A harsh and unforgiving society with unequal bench marks, that pretends we all have equal chances and choices from the start. Benchmarks set by people who may, themselves, have lied or covered up or chosen to ignore serious crimes.

Learning to understand and differentiate social comparisons and understanding that complexity with an ambiguous set of standards has come with age. I've had the advantage of experiencing many different social experiences throughout my life. Even though I am only forty-four years old at the time of writing this book, I understand the hearts and minds of many people who make up our society in many different ways.

The young girl growing up in difficult circumstances in a poor background; the young mother striving to become working class; the incarcerated and shamed; middle class and educated; social stigma and loneliness; I've experienced them all and from each, I hold a deeply philosophical and compassionate approach to all who remain in those circumstances, because I have suffered and experienced deep pain too.

To be hugely underestimated and misunderstood in your integrity and values and to be held accountable for actions that you had very little control over does almost kill you. For now, I strive to raise awareness of how, perhaps where a person comes from, or what their experiences have been, are less important than their heart or intentions for others.

The journey has been a difficult and painful one; the lessons have had to be tough to help me understand. My pride shattered before I was humbled. Forgiveness has had to be vast before I was able to consider forgiving. My compassion for others came at a painful price.

The most shocking lesson for me was the realisation there were, and *are*, hundreds like me, even thousands, most of whom had something lacking in their early life which forged decisions that shaped their future.

Many of the women I met along my path suffered from deep anxiety and depression; women who were starkly isolated in prisons, which often have no visible bars; they internalise mistakes they, themselves, and others have made, and as a result have come to believe they do not deserve any chance again in the future.

I write this book for both men and women alike who are, like me, the hidden, the hopeless and many who have the potential to be our future, but for now, remain without a voice. I dedicate this book to all of you.

Chapter 1

It was early, bordering mid morning, and I was standing in a cell looking into a small plastic mirror, trying to see my reflection clearly, feeling overly conscious about my appearance. I always felt self-conscious when I looked in the mirror. It was almost as though I couldn't bear to see the woman looking back. I took on everything everyone had told me in my life, despite my desperate will to hold on to and believe in myself.

My battle remained a continual struggle with constant oppression. It had come to the point I could no longer look at my own face comfortably; I cringed when I looked in the mirror, my whole body cringed and I held my face tight. I wasn't even fully aware of it, then. There were so many labels I was wearing and even in this place, where so many people were also judged, I still held a stigma and one particular label that was different to, and worse than, everyone else.

Yes, I was different to the others and today in particular, there was nothing I could do or say to myself to feel better. I needed reassurance from someone, but there was not one person here, not one person I could call upon for comfort, to tell me everything was going to be OK, or just to be strong.

I moved the small plastic mirror onto the window ledge to see my reflection more clearly; I was intensely worried about my appearance and what my image might portray today. But this was not a concern born of vanity.

Does my hair down make me look dishonest or honest? I thought.

I wanted the person I was preparing to meet that day to see I was a genuine and honest person. I wanted them to see the person inside, the real me. I knew it was difficult for most to see past the huge label I carried.

It was a pointless and impossible task to explain that label to those I met and to ask them to see past it, so I wouldn't. Coping with other people's perceptions of me caused a constant pain in my heart. It hurt so much; I knew I wasn't deserving of *that* label, and I wasn't capable of any sort of act which harmed another human being, especially my father.

Many people I'd met over the years commented that my hair was beautiful but I had learned to hide it, as I had also heard many vicious remarks. So I looked at my obscured reflection and tied my hair back to take away any attention from it. The reason I hid it today was more than appropriate dress code; it was because I didn't want to invoke another label – that of being "manipulative."

In fact, the way the label *manipulative* was used with reference to me was something that was never specifically explained to me. *What did manipulative really mean? Was it meant to imply that I was controlling, deceptive or cunning?* I never understood.

Most of the time, I believed I was selfless, giving over and beyond to others, far more than I ever did for myself. Everyone used to like me. I drew people in like a magnet; I gave my heart out and believed in everyone. I gave much of myself away and that was why the label *manipulative* being applied to me, ate at me from the inside out, like a cancer. My once wide-open heart was now shut and locked tight.

Over the years, the constant repetition and accusation of being manipulative had done grave damage; I no longer trusted what I knew and I was afraid, if people liked me, it might have been because I was being unknowingly manipulative – I *still* didn't understand what that meant in relation to the person I believed I was.

So I hid my hair as a reaction to so many years of being analysed as manipulative as if, somehow, my very hair proved the analyses.

Nothing could adequately or properly articulate the unspoken terror that somehow, the label might be true; how could I know for sure, when I had no idea how other people's perceptions interpreted me as manipulative?

Today was an important day; the day that marked the first day of the rest of my second chance in life. I tied my hair back in the hope that the person I was going to meet would only see my heart and see that, beyond the entire stigma and label of being manipulative, I was a good person and deserved another chance.

I had had to watch with horror as the rest of my family struggled to continue their lives without me, needing me there to put things right.

But this was never ever going to be able to be put right or have any sense of reason or logic to me.

Lives had been destroyed.

Childhoods were destroyed.

The pain continued.

And today I had to ask someone, despite that impact, to give me another chance.

I put on my make-up, the seriousness of the coming situation evident on my tightly held face. I was preparing to explain *again* the act of a stranger on one horrific day, at the end of a six-week period, some fourteen years earlier.

Worse, I'd be expected to explain that act as if it were mine, and how, at the age of twenty-two years old, I did not prevent another's action.

It was something even they could not explain, something that no one could see, or hear, or touch – in spite of all the demands for explanations from me, no one had ever said exactly how I was supposed to have manipulated another person, or group of circumstances, to cause the unimaginable destruction of that day.

I was young, inexperienced and naïve – far from being a psychologist – how could I know how to describe different reactions to trauma? All that was clear was one life was taken and I often wished that it was mine, in an act of heroism to save his precious life.

The real word to describe me, I believed, and which I could not get away from, was a *coward*. Yes, *a coward*, my internalised messages accused: *You deserve everything you get.*

Again, I glanced in the mirror and saw empty eyes looking back at me. The young woman, the one I was about to speak for, was no longer here. She was dead and had died all those years ago.

I had been cruel and called her a coward over and over. But I still remembered how her naivety and vulnerability used to reflect back in the mirror. Those eyes belonged to a different lifetime, and all the experiences that went with it. The longing for acceptance and belonging I had once yearned for was gone, lost knowing that the label I wore made it no longer attainable. The empty eyes stared back at me, reminding me of all that was lost.

The things I'd seen since, and the harsh lessons that hardened a once soft and gentle heart prepared me for only one thing: survival.

To survive was a promise I made to myself when I was twenty-nine, after years of trying to come to terms with the loss of my father. It was hard to accept the cruel fate that crossed my life's path. That thought was with me continually as the centre voice of my soul, which quietened in my middle agedness, as I gradually came to an acceptance of its presence. *It wasn't fair*; of course it wasn't fair, but if I were to survive, I had to find a way forward.

I had to come to the acceptance that it wasn't my life that was taken, and there had to be a reason for that. I was still here, and I knew I had to do something with that. My daughter needed me and my truth; the real truth had to be heard. It couldn't be heard here, with all the labels and prejudices, but somewhere, somehow, it could and would be heard and that could only happen if I survived to tell it.

The inner ache never left my heart. Despite my promise to survive, I had no love of, or will for, this life, and it showed in my eyes. I had to work so hard to try and conceal the emptiness. It was the only way to be able to leave this place and begin another chapter, another life.

Here and now, I lived to tell the tale and was about to re-live and recall it, to tell a stranger of my achievements since that day and explain to that stranger how I have *changed*.

It was true, I had changed, but the real changes they could never know or comprehend. I had learned to survive a breakdown in an institution and had hidden it the best way I could, because a breakdown and its consequences were not the sort of change they wanted to see.

I couldn't explain that my mind could not cope rationally with witnessing the most horrific act possible – the official story was that I had somehow manipulated that act into existence – against that backdrop, a breakdown and its consequences made no sense, even though, in reality, it did all make perfect sense.

Being innocent of *any* wrongdoing made a mental collapse inevitable. When your truth clashes with an officially decided *truth*, how can you ever be heard or understood?

So, I was going to tell the stranger the truth.

I didn't realise that I did not *allow* these things to happen. I was so damaged by the whole experience, I still did not fully understand that the decisions and actions of another human being were not my responsibility; they were not within my control.

I walked over to the resettlement unit, where I would meet the person who had the power to give me my freedom. Although the day was a significant one for me, everyone else was getting on with their activities around me, like it was a day that did not matter, which of course, it was for them.

It would not affect any of the other women I shared this institution with. This was what an institution was all about; a place full of strangers and women who shared a time of your life.

The wing cleaner looked up at me because I looked different, dressed inappropriately for prison and more like a job interview. I could see her puzzled expression before she looked back down at her mop, already moving on in her mind.

I stood out and I knew I looked extremely nervous. It raised some bored faces, their expressions changing slightly, momentarily, from the usual look of blank disinterest. 'Same thing different day' was the general look I was used to. If you have ever watched the movie *Groundhog Day*, that repetition is the experience of prison life; it just becomes harder and harder the longer you are incarcerated.

Today, however, was different. The day was finally here, the only reason I had chosen to wake every morning for the last fourteen years.

This was the day that I had once thought I would never have

to experience, because I had hoped for appeal many years earlier. I believed that someone would save me from a fate that was out of my control and be able to explain that to any reasonable court of law. But no! Years had passed until *they* were ready to decide I had been punished enough. This day, I had to tell them of my actions or inactions and they would make a decision whether or not to give me my freedom once again.

I walked into the prepared room, sat down and glanced up at the stranger sitting opposite me. He raised his head and looked momentarily surprised, in a good way, I thought. I felt his flash of positive surprise had to be a good sign.

However, I was careful not show what I perceived and used the safe, blank expression which I had learned to use over the years to disguise my perceptions and reactions. No reaction is better than any reaction, good or bad, in prison; either can be over-analysed or misunderstood. I had had to learn to blend in and keep my head down, not to get too involved with others, in case it might lead to tension, all of it for this one day. Just to be able to finally go home to my daughter and try to make things right for her.

I'd kept my head down, I'd studied for weeks in my room, planning and swotting for this day. I knew early on that I would be on the bottom of the social ladder when I was released. I planned to do everything I could for this day, to put myself in the best position possible to at least have a small amount of success. I heard my heart beating faster; it was so loud I thought everyone else would have heard it too. I knew I had support in that room – there were people who had listened to my pain over the years and believed me.

One professional woman had previously stated: "I find it painful to watch Michelle recount the event, she is obviously a traumatised woman and is suffering from deep distress."

There were people in that room that desperately wanted me to have a second chance.

The judge sitting across from me seemed powerful. He had a strong air about him and when he spoke, he was very direct, clear and loud. He started by asking questions about the murder of my father in September 1993. It was a story I knew had gaps and I could only ever explain part of it.

It would have been easier to explain if people had asked the right questions like, 'What were you doing there at the time?' or 'How did you and your father come to be driven out to a remote place by someone you had both only known for six weeks?'

The gaps in the story were created by the questions being asked; when a question begins by stating you did this, this and this, why? The answer is based on assumption. That you did, in fact, do those things – if you didn't, you can't adequately answer the question – and this became a central factor in the misunderstandings that had led me to where I was today.

For example, I was not able to answer the question, 'Why did you kill your father?'

The answer was simple; *I didn't.*

But, there was no way of having that answer heard or accepted, since the implication already was that *I* did kill my father. Instead of saying that, I skirted around it and took responsibility for the only action I did take – nothing.

"I was a young girl," I answered. "I was a young girl and now I am a thirty-eight-year-old woman. I'm responsible for not stopping the murder of my father. For that I am sorry and I am sorry that I cannot change it."

More questions were fired as if to try and trip me up. The judge put it to me that I had killed my father because I was sick of him and had come to the end of my patience with all his substance misuse.

I did not and had not.

I cried and said, "I'm sorry, that is not true."

I stuck to the truth, which was all I knew. I loved my father. I worshiped him and the painful truth that killed me was that I hadn't stopped a mad man from committing murder.

I had come to believe that it had been bizarre behaviour on my part, allowing myself to be stuck in the back seat of a two-door car, incapable of stopping a horrific journey and its final destination.

The judge looked frustrated and his voice became louder.

The psychologist in the room defended me, "Michelle has been repeating the same story for years. The scenario of being in a strange relationship with someone she had only known for six weeks was out of character for Michelle, it was not her character to commit this act and if we keep her in for another twenty years I'm not sure what good it will do, she will tell the same story."

The judge settled down and looked at me with a deep gaze, using a voice that I will never forget, as if to pick up the woman he had clearly killed, again, as she sat there silent with tears rolling down her face. The mask of being alive had gone and my hope had vanished.

"I did not stop it from happening," was the last thing I heard myself say, as if to profess my guilt. "It was my guilt and I can never take it back."

The judge's eyes bore into mine as if to speak to my soul and not my physical presence. Had he been testing me, pushing to get to the real, final, total truth. If he had, then he succeeded. All of the protective fronts were gone. All that sat before him was me, as I was, as I had always been.

He said, with firm authority and power, "It is not a crime NOT to stop something from happening."

He said it as if he wanted me to remember it. My head started spinning – I was so confused.

I had told them over and over that I was sorry and was a different person, yet here I was, doing exactly the same again, after paying the price of losing my life and losing out on so much, only to be told those words, after all these years.

It is not a crime NOT to stop something from happening.

Why had it taken this long? How did a gentle person like me get to be here, carrying the burdens of another's actions and carrying guilt for it, which was never mine to carry?

Chapter 2

"Daddy. Daddy," I screamed, running through the neglected and overgrown garden.

Our house stood on the corner of the street on a generous sized plot with front, side and back garden. Some of its flowers and weeds were literally as tall as me and my heart pounded as I pushed them to one side to get to my father as quickly as I could.

My face was wet with a mixture of perspiration and tears. It had been a considerably hot summer and I had spent most of the time playing in the garden alone or with my friends. This particular day, I had been in the back garden of a girl who lived across the road from me, looking through the bushes for ladybirds. That summer had brought a swarm of them and I carried a small jam jar with holes in its lid to capture a variety of ladybirds and other insects for pets. That's when I ended up falling into the nettle patch, trying to balance on the uneven, hard and bumpy soil, reaching out to capture a creature.

I was completely stunned at first and looked up to see my friend's horrified faces, before feeling intense stabbing pains across my body. Instinctively, I got up and ran. I ran to the wooden gate, which was locked to keep us safely in the garden, and I pressed the metal latch down to make an exit that was not normally allowed. I ran across the road and through our back garden, trying to get to my father as fast as I could. Only he could make it better.

Nothing and no one could stop me; I ignored my friends even though they shouted and attempted to stop me from running out onto the road.

"Michelle," they yelled, "Rub a dock leaf on it."

It was no use. I needed more than dock leaves. I needed to feel the comfort and the safety of my father to feel better.

He was standing in the middle of the kitchen when I reached the open back door. My father exuded warmth in everything from his physical appearance to the loving energy surrounding him. It was a fair opinion of many in the community that I absolutely idolised him. In fact, my mother told many people that I would kiss the ground he walked on.

He was slightly built, with a moustache that curled up at the corners when he smiled. His most significant feature was his auburn hair, long, wavy and shiny.

Lifting me into the air, he looked into my eyes as I sobbed.

"What happened?" he asked, gently. I pointed to my bare legs that were now covered in a bumpy rash.

He sat me on the top of one of the kitchen cupboards.

"It's going to be ok," he said, "I have just the thing to make it better."

He smiled a kind smile and I was instantly reassured. I watched his face closely as he opened a cupboard, taking from it a bottle of pink liquid and some cotton wool. He dabbed the liquid onto my legs and sure enough, just as he had promised, the prickling seemed to ease within minutes. I smiled at him in wonder.

"See!" he said, confirming his earlier promises.

Not only had the pain started to fade but also, my heart had been comforted from its shock from the fall in a moment of his presence.

"I want you home in one hour," my Dad told me firmly, before my feet touched the floor.

"OK," I shouted, half way to the door, running as fast as I could.

This time I ran in excitement – it had occurred to me that while I was here getting better, I had missed out on collecting ladybirds and other insects and I needed to get back to my friends as quickly as I could, before our time together and the day came to an end.

In our family home, I spent most of my time with my father. My mother worked as a waitress and a cleaner in a local hotel near the seafront. She would often leave the house early in the morning and didn't return until much later in the day.

Spending time with my father was something that brought me much happiness. He had a multitude of roles and one of those was teaching me many exciting things about subjects such as nature, insects, and animals. My brother and I even had the privilege of staying up late with my father some evenings, sitting under the stars naming them and spotting meteorites.

"Did you see it?" he would ask in excitement, as we sat in the garden watching a bright light disappear in a minuscule of a second flash across the sky.

"Yes, yes," I'd tell him and then, when the show was over, he would go back to his small blue book of digits and dates to predict the next one.

Some nights, however, were not always as successful and he would stare disappointedly into the sky while we looked at him, waiting for the show to start.

"It's no good at all," he would say, as if to himself.

"Why Dad?" I would ask, "Let's wait a little longer." I wanted to reassure him that we were interested in his knowledge just as much as he was.

Even at that young age, I had learned to watch his face for disappointment, in order to say something reassuring in return.

"No, no it's far too cloudy, we're not going to see anything at all," he'd say, always genuinely disappointed.

The summer of my fifth year, he taught me many names of insects, which had initiated my search for, and collection of them. When I first started keeping them in a jam jar, my father shook his head.

"You can't keep the insects in there," he told me, when he saw me carrying it about.

"Why?" I asked, getting upset. "I want to keep my insects."

He took the jam jar temporarily from me and returned it to me now with holes poked through the metal lid.

"Put some leaves in it," he told me, "they have nothing to eat in there. Let them go at the end of the day and collect new ones the following day."

"Why?" I asked.

"Well," he went on to explain, "some insects only live for three days and by keeping them in the jam jar, you've kept them in there for a third of their lives."

I understood and absorbed the lesson of empathy for all things that he had just taught so gently.

I didn't really understand my mother as well as my father. Her character was the opposite in a lot of ways, particularly with me. Although I had a loving bond towards her, it didn't appear to be reciprocal. She spoke more often to my brother, but in an exaggeratedly loving way.

She was both cold and aggressive when she spoke to me and only looked happy when she mimicked me to the point of almost laughing at me when she saw me upset, as though she was trying to torment my emotions.

"Why don't you like me?" I asked her one-day. I could feel a negative energy from her in the kitchen, while I sat waiting for my tea.

"I do like you," she replied.

"You don't, I can feel it," I answered her. I couldn't have explained any further – all I knew was that I could *feel* her displeasure at my presence.

"You can't feel whether someone likes you or not," she sneered.

I thought about what she had said and started to doubt whether what I was feeling was the actual truth – it felt so real.

I turned to my father, hurt and confused, looking to him for reassurance. His face beamed at me as he walked in and placed a pile of knives and forks in the middle of the table. The table wobbled as I put the knives and forks in their correct places, so he put a small, folded square of cardboard under one of the shorter legs, stopping it from wobbling.

I sat down at the table and tilted my chair back.

"Don't tip your chair back onto two legs," he said, watching me as I balanced, holding the wobbly table for support.

"Why?" I asked, placing the chair back onto its four legs. "I won't fall."

My mother answered instead. "You will bloody crack your head open...and don't ask why, just do as you're told, you little monster."

I didn't get hurt physically, but my mother's harsh words crushed me. She shouted so loudly, she didn't appear as concerned about my head as she was about her own shouting.

"Come on, Son," she said in a softer tone to my brother Neil, as he walked into the kitchen. In an instant, she sounded like a completely different person. In fact, she sounded like a soft, compassionate, loving and giving woman. Neil sat down at the table and gazed at her with a look equally as hostile as the one she gave to me. He appeared to be uncomfortable with her exaggerated fussiness and eagerness to please him.

I smiled at my older brother as he sat down. He returned my love with a straight face. I looked at his face, analysing it; I felt his expression was more of an act – I was sure that he loved me.

My concentration was broken as my father placed our favourite picture plates in front of us. Smiling at me, he then covered the pictures with the smoking stew. I looked at my brother in anticipation of a race. Dinnertime for my brother and me when eating from these plates became a game to see who could make the pictures reappear first, then clean off the plate with bread. I picked up my spoon before my father had finished dishing out the stew and began to eat. I spooned up more of the stew before I had even swallowed the mouthful before, in order to eat it as quickly as I could.

My mother shouted angrily again, glaring at me. "You're going to bloody choke, stop now."

I couldn't stop or else my brother would win. I looked up at his face only a minute later and his huge, smug smile told me his plate was empty.

"It's not fair," I cried out.

"Don't speak to your brother like that," my mother shouted again, her tone hostile. I didn't understand why she was asking me not to speak to my brother like this, when I couldn't have spoken to him as loudly or as angrily as she spoke to me.

Losing competitions to my brother was nothing new. He always won! One of his favourite games was holding some straws in his closed hand and asking me to pull one out.

"Pick out the longest," he'd say, beaming a huge, teasing smile. I fell for it every time, picking the one which appeared the longest, only then to watch in defeat as he went on to pull out the one which seemed shorter at first, but had a much longer length hidden in his hand. I ran to my father, who now became my advisor.

"Dad," I shouted, "it's not fair."

My father challenged my young mind. "You have to think Michelle, it's a trick."

On other days, there were competitions of strength, like the arm wrestles that he always used to win, too. I was determined to win at this game, always demanding another go when I had been beaten continually.

I didn't understand strength in terms of the physical, but only in will. I knew that I willed myself to win this game with him so much that my will itself didn't want to give up.

"Ok, ok," he grinned, "I tell you what, I'll give you a chance this time."

He held his arm again, this time by forty-five degrees in my favour. I looked at his face and thought of him as a fool. I smiled at him, knowingly – I was surely going to win with this chance. My arm was nearly in the winning position! I pushed his arm with all my might but my arm couldn't go the short distance and was stuck in mid-air. Then, much to my dismay, my arm was being pushed in the opposite direction and was in the central position; what's more, my brother didn't even look like he was trying. Neil smiled one of his huge smiles as he pushed down my arm with ease to the other side of the table, winning the competition again.

"Boys are stronger than girls," he teased, explaining his superior strength.

"It's not true," I yelled and again ran to my father.

"This time, Michelle," my father explained, "Neil is right; boys are physically stronger, but girls can be mentally stronger than boys and sometimes, in life, that is what really counts."

I looked at him, not convinced.

"I'm mentally stronger," I said to Neil. He didn't look the slightest bit interested and had now moved on to playing another game. The novelty of being mentally stronger quickly wore off.

The house we lived in was run down. The walls were lined with unpainted woodchip wallpaper. I'd been told off several times for picking at the chips where I often sat and pondered on the bottom rung of the stairs. The carpet was thin and thread bare. Our sofa was worn and dipped in the middle; if I sat on it alone, I would sink in, unable to get out until someone sat in the other seat, rebalancing me so I could move. What I loved most about our home was the smell of the blankets as my father tucked me up in bed at night. That smell made me feel safe and I associated it with the security my father gave me.

My Dad would often pretend not to notice when he tucked me in at night that he had covered my head when he threw the blankets over me.

"Whoops," he would laugh, as if it had been a genuine mistake.

"Daddy!" I'd squeal, as my face disappeared. He always kissed me goodnight and left me feeling safe to sleep before he went downstairs. Sometimes, I would hear my parents arguing before I drifted off to sleep.

(One night, I had a dream that my bed was falling downstairs and out of the front door into the street. I always recalled my dreams to my Dad because they frightened me and his face was serious, as if it signalled an omen. Just like the staircase dream, I knew he didn't understand what brought me such night terrors, all I knew was that he listened with loving concern.)

The arguing increased…soon it seemed like every night and over the weeks, it started to leak into the days as well. I walked into the living room one-day, knowing the argument was more serious than usual. My father sat, gripping both arms of the armchair tightly. My mother stood closely by him, talking with a serious voice.

Neil was standing in the doorway, frozen – it was the first time I saw him looking so frightened. He had heard the whole conversation and he put his arm round me for assurance.

My father was taking a strong stance, firmly saying, "No, you're not, Denise."

"Yes, I am, Keith, I'm taking them both," her voice was adamant.

I held on to Neil and looked up at him.

"She won't," he comforted. The words horrified us – we both knew our father to be our nurturer.

"Oh yes, I am, Keith, I'm taking them both," she fought again.

She looked like she meant it. *Go where?* I didn't want to go anywhere with her. Somehow, I knew what this conversation meant. If anyone had asked me to choose who I wanted to live with, it would have been an easy decision, even though I was young, I would have undoubtedly chosen my father who made me feel safe, rather than my mother who made me unsure of myself and afraid to speak to her.

Why did she want to take me from my father anyway? I wondered. It didn't make any sense when I loved him so much and he loved me.

My father shouted back, "You're not taking either of them," as if he was fighting for his life.

"I am Keith," It was a cold statement of certainty.

19

In spite of his strong stance, my father looked scared, like she had some kind a hold over him. The reason for that I was to learn a little later in my life.

In the weeks that followed, we settled into a new kind of normality. My mother wasn't around any more. She had gone to my Dad's cousin, Aunty Anne, in the meantime, asking for help. For a short time, everything seemed OK.

Then Aunty Anne, a strong-willed, formidable woman, spoke her words of wisdom – there was no mistaking that she expected to be obeyed.

'The mother should take the girl, and the father should keep the boy', she had stated, as a compromise to my father keeping us both, or my mother taking us both. It made no sense at all to me. In fact, it would have made more sense for my mother to take my brother, the child she cared for.

I held on to my brother again for reassurance when my mother returned.

"It's going to be OK," he said, bravely trying to cover his fear. That's when I knew that I was leaving. I was leaving with the mother who stared at me coldly, who acted like she had hated me. The mother who mimicked me when I spoke, the mother I didn't know and with whom I couldn't communicate.

All because an aunty, who had some kind of authority in the family, had said so. *Who was she anyway?* I couldn't remember her visiting our house or understanding our family; in fact, I don't remember ever meeting her at all before that day.

I didn't want to be taken away from my father. I felt helpless, hopeless and powerless. I was as afraid that day as I was in the middle of the worst of my nightmares.

My mother looked as hopeless as I did, if not more so. She looked longingly at my brother, then, took me in his place. It seemed that my father was lucky to have kept Neil – again, I somehow knew he'd come close to losing us both.

Losing Neil was something that my mother was clearly distraught over. Walking out of the house with her into the dark cold night, not knowing where I was going, I knew the loss of my brother had crushed her.

"Don't cry mummy," I said, trying, to comfort her.

She was physically crying, walking around the corner from our home.

"Shut up, you little monster," she snapped at me.

I felt as though she was taking her pain and loss out on me. I stopped speaking. I had to swallow the hurt down in my throat before she had the chance to mimic my emotions. I held back the tears by tilting my head back a little, so they wouldn't roll down my cheek and she wouldn't notice.

I had no father to run to; I started to feel very alone as we walked in the darkness to my new home.

Chapter 3

My mother's and my relationship, no longer overseen by my father, began to get worse. I am sure it didn't help my mother all that much that I constantly asked to see him. At first, I held my mother to the promises I had been given to persuade me to leave my father.

"You can come and see me whenever you want," he promised.

"Every day, then," I gasped. That was, of course, exactly how often I wanted to see him.

"Yes," he laughed, delighted that was what I wanted.

My mother seemed to know something about him, something I was not allowed to know. I often used to hear the tail end of a conversation or a snippet of a word when I walked in the living room door unexpectedly. The sudden, strange hush made the situation much worse and I demanded to know what was wrong. I wasn't sure at all about it, but it made me feel like something was wrong with my father. It made me worry about him.

Was he sick? I would think to myself. It was always my father who reassured me that everything was OK.

So, I reminded my mother of those agreements every day, from the day that I had left.

"Can I see my Dad today?"

"I'm just finishing the washing off," my mother replied, politely, without turning to look at me.

"After you've finished then?"

"Yes, later, I will take you," my mother replied.

I felt a mixture of both disappointment and excitement. The answer was always a 'yes, but not yet'. It seemed like over the days and weeks that followed my mother was always busy. Before I knew it, I would be waiting for tomorrow to come again. It didn't stop me from asking, though. On one of those days when I was waiting to see him, it suddenly started to dawn on me that I might not see him today, but also, tomorrow may never come either. I couldn't bear to wait another day. I decided that day that I was going to plead with my mother in the hope that she might change her mind.

I climbed the stairs to the flat from the garden where I had been playing.

"You're taking me to see my Dad today?" I reminded her when I reached the kitchen, only this time, with a questioning tone rather than a reminding statement.

My mother had seemed patient so far with my requests, but today that patience had disappeared.

"I know," she snapped, "I forgot."

"Can I go now then?" I pleaded.

"No," she said firmly, "I'm busy."

I couldn't hide my disappointment from her any longer. I left the flat and went back downstairs into the yard. From the garden, I looked up to the small kitchen window on the second floor and tried to judge whether my mother could see me or not. I had already come to the conclusion when I was half way down the stairs that today, I would make the first big decision on my own in the entirety of my short life.

I knew exactly where my father lived from the flat and I was going to see him today, by myself. I had stayed for hours in the garden on my own before today and if I went to see my Dad that minute, I could probably make it back before she even noticed I was gone.

I walked out of the back garden and turned left into the dark alleyway. My heart started to beat louder. I then turned right to walk out onto the busy high street.

Nobody look at me, I willed people passing by me in my mind.

I looked down at the floor, hoping that this way, no one would notice me. I knew the way, it was easy, but the hardest part would be crossing the busy road. I spoke to myself in my mind to give me courage.

Don't look at anyone while you cross, they just might stop you.

I crossed safely, turned left and ran through a courtyard, passing a pub which my father had taken me to once. He had seated me on a high bar stool, where I was introduced to the bar man, like he had come first in a competition and I was his prize. Running through that same courtyard now, I wished I were sitting on that bar stool with my dad. I ran as fast as I could to the end of the yard, where the big black steel gates were open. I ran straight through them to the houses on the small council estate where my father now lived with my brother, the place that had not so very long ago been my home.

My best friend, Tim, shouted and waved to invite me over to play as I passed. I ignored him. As much as I missed his friendship, I had to get to my father's house, only two streets away. I counted down the seconds in my head to comfort myself, knowing that when I reached to zero, I would have reached his door.

*Ten, nine, eight, seven, six, five, four, three, two…*I felt as though at any point, something or someone might just whisk me up and take me back to the flat.

When I finally arrived at his house, my old home, I took a moment to proudly look up at the big, blue back door. I had made it! Reaching up to the glass window, I knocked as hard as I could, but it didn't sound half as loud as I had wanted it to.

I heard his voice inside. My heart was instantly warmed and I couldn't wait for him to open the door. I would feel loved again and that empty space inside me would be filled.

"That's funny," I could hear his voice, "I am sure I could hear a knock." He was talking to someone in the house.

I began to panic. He didn't even know I was here. He couldn't see my silhouette through the glass window of the door, as I wasn't tall enough to reach past the wooden panel at the bottom half of it. I knocked again, this time with more force. Just after I did, that initial doubt and panic started to rise, as I stood there waiting for him to open it. I was probably going to be in big trouble from my mother and those consequences were now starting to come to the forefront of my mind.

Was it better for me to turn around now before she realised I'd gone? I turned around to run and at that very second, the door opened.

"Oh, no you don't," I heard that soft voice teasing. I turned and beamed. Here he was.

"Daddy," I said, "I've been trying to see you."

He opened his arms to lift me up, giving me a huge hug. Into the warm home I went and after I sat down, I recounted the days of asking my mother to take me to see him.

"She keeps saying soon," I told him, realising she had never meant it.

"I knew she would be back Keith, right where she belongs." A dark haired man, who'd been sitting at the table in the living room, was speaking – I couldn't remember seeing him before.

The man smiled proudly at me.

"I had better go, Mum will wonder where I am," I said to him, the reality of the consequences of her noticing I was gone now crowding into my brain.

"Oh, no you don't," he smiled. "Your mother will know exactly where you are."

Enjoying my father's company, I waited for my mother to come and collect me. We talked together for what seemed like hours and he made me laugh again and again. When my mother finally walked in through the back door, it was just turning dark. My father was right. She knew where I would be. He was always right, only it was much later than he had expected her. Everything he said was the truth. I looked at him with awe. I wanted to be like him. I loved him so much.

"I am sorry Keith," my mother said, exaggeratedly, when my father asked her about how long I'd been gone.

She didn't know if it was for half an hour or all day. My father kept questioning her about the length of time it took her to notice I had gone.

"She was safe Keith, in the garden."

I watched my mother try to convince my father of her care for me, knowing that it was all just a pretence.

My mother had recently told me, out of the blue, about her loss of another child before I was conceived. She said that if she had had the child, she would have never have had another. Maybe that grief affected the way she treated me. I didn't know; I was too young to understand. I only knew I sought her love constantly, but couldn't seem to do anything to gain it.

I was pushing my doll in its pram down the busy high street towards our flat when she told me. I recall looking down at my doll, who I loved so much, all wrapped up in a warm blanket; I looked up at my own mother's cold face. How must she feel, I thought, not wanting me, but having to look after me?

"Mum, I am really sorry I was born," I told her.

I truly wished I hadn't been born, to give her some happiness in that moment. I loved her and wanted her to be happy, but it seemed my presence was making her incredibly sad. More than anything, I desperately needed her love.

"It's OK," she replied. "I get more money for having you."

"You do?" I exclaimed.

I smiled at her and felt a strange kind of happiness. In fact, I thought that I had resolved a problem, which was always in the air. I hoped that I had cleared it in my young mind, just like my father had taught to compromise and understand. If only it had been that easy. I doubted the forgiveness when she squeezed my hand taking me home that night from my fathers.

What confused me most about my mother though was not the rejection, as much as that hurt me, but the different personalities she had when other people were around.

The warm voice she had used for my father was gone now as we walked home in the dark. She was holding my hand, squeezing it so tightly, I couldn't help but cry out in pain. Once again, she mimicked my emotions,

"Boo hoo, hoo," she taunted in a childish voice, mocking my own.

And what was worse, when I told her I loved her, which I often did when she was rejecting me, she would repeat it back to me like a baby, mimicking my voice and laughing as though it was a weak and pathetic thing to say.

"Don't you ever do that again or next time, you'll be wishing you hadn't been born...don't bother running to your father. Do you think he's going to believe you? Well, think again, because he isn't. Adults believe adults, not children. Children are liars, they make things up and not one person, including your father, is going to believe you," she scowled.

It was a bleak moment and hopelessness welled up in me. It was getting much darker, reminding me of the night we left a month or so ago.

"Sorry, Mum," I now attempted to plead. I *was* truly sorry.

I was sorry for myself, knowing I was not going back to my father's. I looked up to see where Tim had been playing – he was now long gone. I'd lost everything. My father, my brother and my friends. I felt huge grief and loneliness for the first time in my life, unaware that my mother might have felt the same feelings as I was feeling, albeit for different people.

Back inside the flat, I wandered to my bedroom alone. I had sat here alone, often for long hours during the past days and weeks. That pattern was to continue in the following months and even years ahead of me. An empty void inside me grew, causing me an emotional pain that I didn't know how to put into words. I sometimes sat in my room for so long that I forgot where I was. My mind would drift off into another world and when I came back, a whole afternoon or day had gone by. I drifted into my own make believe worlds. I had no one for comfort, apart from the teddies lying on my bed. I put myself to bed, moving them up to make room for me. No one else was here.

No one was there to listen to me and the quietness of the flat began to engulf me again. I was being pulled into a vacuum, becoming lost in some kind of huge, empty void.

4

Chapter 4

"Michelle, Michelle," I could hear my teacher's voice coming into my consciousness. Realising my surroundings, I started to focus upon the teacher's face, suddenly aware that she was standing right in front of my desk, looking straight at me.

"Are you OK?" she asked, gently, when she had regained my attention. "Where have you been?"

I turned to my friend Katherine sitting next to me. I was confused and needed her reassurance.

"She's just daydreaming, Miss," Katherine answered for me, and as the young teacher walked back to the front of the class she continued, "She does it a lot."

Katherine glared at me. "What are you doing? Concentrate," she whispered, like an older sister trying to protect a sibling from being in trouble.

Katherine had become my closest friend. I looked up at the young teacher and her colleague, who were now talking quietly at the front of the classroom, looking over at me.

At the end of that very same afternoon, when my mother came to pick me up, the friendly teacher took my mother to one side.

"Just wait there a minute, Michelle, I want a quick word with your Mum," she explained, giving me a book and returning me to my desk.

After they finished speaking, she smiled a huge, kind smile at my mother and me as we left for home. Walking past our flat, I soon realised that we were on our way to my father's. My mother seemed happier than normal, but didn't share the reason for her happiness with me. She just laughed out loud to herself every couple of minutes. I was pleased she was happy.

When we arrived at my father's, she had hardly stepped into the back door before blurting out loudly, with an air of smugness, "Keith, Keith, Michelle has got a learning difficulty, Keith."

It was as if she couldn't wait to tell him the news. I wondered if she was telling him I was no longer worthy of his love.

"No, she hasn't, Denise, and don't say things like that in front of her, it will affect her; can't you see she is taking it all in."

My mother was not defeated by this and continued to explain the conversation that she and the teacher had had, when she came to pick me up from school that afternoon. It all started to make sense to me; the teachers had been worried about me, it seemed, for some time now. Listening to the conversation between my mother and father, I either wasn't listening in class, or wasn't able to take things in. It was like I was drifting off into my own world.

"She's just daydreaming, Denise, I have seen her do it and what do they know?" my father said, dismissively. "They have just walked out of university and know nothing about her. I bet they don't even speak to her, because if they had spoken to her, they would know she is intelligent."

Was there something wrong with me? I always felt confused when I heard my mother talking about me like this in a jovial way, when she should have been concerned and not happy. Her tone had changed, like she was now trying to convince him there was something wrong with me. I wished more than anything that I could live with my father, who remained in his protective mode, not budging an inch.

Most of the time I would walk to and from school by myself; it wasn't that far, but it was far enough for the walk to make me feel lonely. The walk led me to compare my family situation to other children and their families, who were often laughing and talking to their parents. It somehow made me feel different. Some of those days, I walked home with my friends and their parents who were going the same way, but more often than not, I took that short journey on my own.

Walking out of those gates, I automatically escaped into some other world for comfort and I had lost control of it. Sometimes people stared at me with a serious face as I walked to and from school, but no one talked to me and I would snap back into reality and loneliness. *Did they wonder why I was on my own, because if they did, then why didn't anyone say anything to me?*

Until one day, on the way home from school, an older boy walked with me. He talked to me kindly, almost like the two teachers who always spoke to me with such affection. I felt like this must be my lucky day – I was no longer alone, I had a friend to walk with. He was a couple of years older than me and I had never seen him before.

"Why do you walk on your own? People are staring at you because they wonder why you're on your own," he explained, as if he was able to read my mind and had come to answer my question.

I looked around and saw other children with their parents looking at me again. Today, though, I was special, as this boy was obviously someone the other kids looked up to. He had an air of self-confidence and self-respect about him that seemed older than his age. He also had a glow around him and looked as though he was someone important. Furthermore, he was talking to me!

"Do you know your alphabet?" he asked me.

"Yes!" I beamed with pride, singing, out loud, the alphabet, which I had learnt in class only that week. "Will you walk with me again?" I asked him, before he left.

"Yes, yes," he smiled. The next day the boy with the kind voice walked with me on my way home again and people looked at me whilst I talked to him.

"Who's she talking to?" I overheard someone say. The boy smiled a concerned smile. A few days later, he smiled in the same loving way, but said to me,

"I can't walk you home any more, but I will be around; I will walk just in front of you."

"Why?" I asked my friend, feeling a huge loss once again.

"It's better for you if I walk in front of you."

I didn't want him to walk in front of me; I wanted him to walk with me. I had a friend for a moment and that moment was short. For a couple of days, I was happy on my walk home. *Did I imagine him? Was my imagination giving me hope?*

I was so keen to go to school I often arrived much earlier than the other kids. The door was open early and I put my coat on my name tag and greeted the teacher. After the initial months, we had begun to build up a relationship and she always looked happy to see me.

"Oh, no you don't," she would tease, blocking my way when I tried to walk past her without speaking. It seemed I had no choice but to become friends with her.

"Good morning, Michelle, nice to see you and I have just the job for you," she would say, most mornings.

I often helped her to set up the class and it gave us the opportunity to talk. At first, I would simply respond with either a yes or no, but as time went on, she gained my trust and I started to feel happy and content around her. I started to feel a warm glow inside of me in her company and I began to talk to her about all sorts of things.

"There is nothing wrong with her," I heard my teacher say to the other teacher. It was like they were pulling me out of my little world, allowing me to begin to feel a sense of belonging.

Something else had changed, too. My mother had a boyfriend. I called him "Uncle Richard." He had commented on how positively I looked forward to school.

"You don't need a coat," he said one morning. "You're like the Ready Brek advert when you go on your way to school."

I was confused.

"You have a glow," he said, looking pleased.

One day, my class had all made lanterns that we could take home and learnt a song together; we'd hold our lanterns up in class and sing, 'This little light of mine, I'm going to let it shine'. As I sang the song, I became happier and happier and actually felt the glow that Richard had spoken about – it was the glow in my heart. Taking the lantern home, I sang the song happily on my own.

"What are you singing?" Richard asked, kindly.

My mother followed Richard into the room – I thought she looked anxious about him talking to me so nicely. She waited while I sang. Then she blew out the pretend light in my lantern. I re-lit the pretend light and started singing again. She blew the light out again. After the third time, I hid my pretend light from her with my hand.

"Don't do that, Denise, it's wrong," Richard told her, in the same protective way my father would.

My mother started to laugh as, encouraged by Richard's words, I lit the pretend light again behind my cupped hand, she moved my hand and blew it out, laughing coldly. I stared up at the hatred in her eyes. I didn't light it again.

Uncle Richard normally visited us at the flat on odd weekends. His visits changed my living conditions, on those occasions, from silence and aggression to inclusion. He would often talk to me when he visited and took us to places like Danes Dyke, a natural beauty site. I even sat on the floor in front of them to watch TV; slowly I began to leave my room and spend more time with them. I grew so fond of him that I squeezed in to sit next to him, like I would with my father. He was as attentive and kind as my father.

"Get away from him," my mother scowled like a jealous child.

I didn't understand.

"Don't speak to her like that, Denise," Uncle Richard chided, almost as if she was the child.

"She's doing it on purpose, so I can't sit next to you," my mother replied, like a petulant toddler.

"Don't be ridiculous, Denise, she's just a little girl who wants to be loved."

My mother sat on the other side of me reluctantly and squashed me in so there was no room for me to move. Uncle Richard smiled down at me, but I knew as soon as he was gone, I was going to be in big trouble. I sat there apprehensively, wishing I hadn't sat on the sofa at all; that togetherness moment was gone and my heart sank.

Trying to communicate with my mother most of the time, I became frozen in case I said or did the wrong thing. It became apparent that 'sorry' wasn't the right response. Trying to help her was never right, sitting on the floor wasn't right. *What could I do to stop her from being angry with me?*

I made it my mission to understand her so that I could learn what to do right, but most of the time, I thought it was best just not to be noticed and before long, no attention had become a better option than any attention. I also tried not to talk to Uncle Richard when he came, so I didn't upset my mother.

"Has the cat caught your tongue?" he would tease.

He would sit with me and read a book; I looked at my mother helplessly, seeing the hostility in her eyes. My hostile and mimicking mother only fully appeared when other people weren't around.

Then, she would leave me crying uncontrollably, silently begging deep inside for her love. "I love you Mummy," was the most I dared say out loud, pleading with my eyes and my heart for her to say it back.

I remembered asking her directly once, "Do you love me?"

She said nothing.

"Please, Mum, do you love me?" I begged.

Her words, when she finally responded, rained down on me like blows. I sobbed hysterically, barely able to breathe through the tears.

"You're nothing and never will be. No one likes you. No one. They just feel sorry for you. They don't like you. Why would anyone like you? You're a nothing piece of shit, scraped up from my shoe."

Any time other people were around, she would explain our clearly fraught relationship by blaming everyone but herself.

"She's so ungrateful and difficult. She's just like her father."

There is nothing I wanted more than my father, who made me feel safe.

Things changed again when my mum brought home my new

baby brother, not long after we moved into the flat. That was the time I felt the first effects of being judged by others.

Visitors, who had come to visit my mother and the new baby, commented on my reluctance to come forward and be part of the celebrations – they couldn't know how terrified I was of saying or doing the wrong thing.

"Michelle's so difficult," she told them, with an exaggerated sigh. Their sympathetic eyes swivelled from my mother's face to gaze strangely at me. I didn't understand their looks, but I knew it meant they were viewing me in some sort of negative way. This new position brought my mother increasing attention and she began to use it all the time with her friends to seek their sympathy.

"Be good for your mother", they would tell me sternly on their way out.

I looked back at them, saying nothing in my confusion. There was nothing in my vocabulary to voice my own truth – that I tried so hard to be good, but it was never enough; by that stage, I had already begun living without a voice.

School had become my sanctuary.

One day, the headmistress spoke to me in her office.

I sat there quietly, stunned by the fact someone was actually asking me about my mum. I didn't know how to answer and a tangle of information formed in my brain when I tried to gather my thoughts; everything was distorted and confused. I couldn't answer.

I had come to believe the words my mother said to me. In my mind, my mum stated the *facts* of who I was – I was nothing – she instilled in me that adults are right and children are liars. Adults believe adults, they don't believe children. Adults always stick together. There was nothing I could tell the headmistress, not because there was nothing *to* tell, but because I had no way of finding the words. Even if I had, I would have been far too afraid to utter them.

Katherine nudged me one day when the teachers were talking at the front of the class. She whispered to me "They're talking about you."

I strained my ears to listen.

"There's nothing wrong with her at all...she is so loving; I don't think her mother even talks to her if she doesn't have to."

"Have you seen her mum?"

"Yes, I don't see her often but when I do she..."

For the first time ever, I was hearing people who were not fooled by my mother's outward loving appearance to the world. I didn't know what to make of it.

Chapter 5

I came to understand, while I was growing up, that my father was different from most other people. I didn't learn this from him, but I learnt it from observing the misconceptions of others around me, coming to understand how he didn't fit into their social expectations.

Others would often look at him and speak about him in ways that divulged their obscured way of thinking. My father would sometimes express his hurt; people even in his own family had disowned him because he didn't fit in and didn't even acknowledge him when they saw him in the street. It seemed like he was a social misfit.

He didn't leave the house all that often and my mother's visits to take me to see him decreased following the birth of my brother.

My father had turned up at our flat occasionally over the next few years, but he was mostly not allowed in and I wouldn't see him.

When my younger brother was about five and I was ten, my relationship with my father was rekindled after what seemed a huge chunk of my life. It came at a time when my mother started to return to work in the local hotel and my father would take care of me and my younger brother.

It had been such a long time since I'd spent any time with my father, I felt as though he was a stranger and acted shy around him.

"Talk to him, then," my mother blurted out, as my faced burned red with shyness, standing in the living room looking at him and feeling out of place in the space I had once called home.

I had spent most of the intervening years playing with my friends out on the estate where I lived with mother. I'd stay out until it was getting dark to be away from my mother for as long as possible. Today was one of those days I would have been with my friends and I thought about them as I looked at my father's hurt face and forced a smile. I was pleased to see him, deep down; however, playing with my friends was, at that moment, at the forefront of my mind.

"She doesn't even know me, Denise," he complained. "Five years is a large gap in a child's life."

Even our reasons for being there were, in truth, nothing to do with allowing me to rebuild my relationship with my dad.

Shortly after my younger brother was born, my mother and he had a tragic accident and at five, he was still in his pushchair because of his mental and physical disabilities. I had cared for him on my own, any time my mother was out, up until this day, but someone had apparently been talking about my mother and threatened to report her to social services for leaving a child with a minor – however, this may, in fact, have been an early indication of her failing mental health. Now he would be taken to my father's every day during the summer holidays, while my mother worked for the local hotel.

And so began a new routine – my mother would walk both of us to my father's every morning in a jolly sort of way, booming her presence with a large *hello* to all the local neighbours.

Everyone seemed to love my mother – she'd stop to chat in an exaggeratedly intimate manner with whoever was out and about.

I soon settled into the new routine, and once again felt cocooned in my father's love.

I loved walking to the local shops with him, holding his hand tightly. He often stopped and talked to the neighbours proudly about me and about how much I had grown. Mavis, my father's neighbour and mother of my long lost friend Tim, was a quietly spoken and gentle woman. She stopped to talk to my mother one day, asking, "How are you, Denise?" as we arrived at my father's house and stood at his gate.

"I'm OK, Mavis," my mother replied, loudly. "I'm just bringing Michelle to see her Dad again…that's all she wants to do… see her Dad. She worships him, you know; she'd kiss the ground he walks on."

Mavis smiled. "Girls often do," she replied.

Mavis examined my face, her eyes concerned.

"Michelle is so quiet," I heard her say, as if she was comparing the introverted older girl standing in front of her with the younger, happier, free spirited one who had left some five years earlier.

Although it hadn't taken long to get used to being with my dad again – in fact, now, given the option, I'd much rather be with him than playing with my friends on the estate – I was troubled by my inability to speak properly to him. There was so much I wanted to say to him, but I didn't seem to know where to start or how to get it out.

"There's nothing wrong with being quiet," he told me kindly, reassuring me that it was OK not to speak.

All I wanted to tell him was that my mother didn't love me and I should return to him for good. He played a song to me on his record player: it was by a band called Pink Floyd, he told me, and the song was called *Keep Talking*. The words reflected my feelings exactly; as

I listened, I realised that he knew my every thought, concern and worry.

Of course, I *could* speak, but I thought intensely before I did about what I was going to say – then, I would become lost – my words weren't joined up and I expected that everyone could understand me when they didn't. My father, however, did.

"It's OK, Michelle," he would smile as I blushed with embarrassment about his apparent awareness of my being *afraid* to speak.

Perhaps it was because I was spending so much time with him again, perhaps because I was older now, or maybe a combination of both, but I had become acutely aware of the level aware of the level of stereotyping levelled at my dad.

We lived in a small town and there weren't many men with long hair. Some of his friends used to have long hair in the sixties, but had long since cut it. I knew this, because they used to reminisce about their own long hair when they saw him, as if my father's hair had stoked up fond memories for them. My Father was a hippy who had loved those times and stayed with them instead of growing into the social norms of the seventies and eighties.

It was on one of those occasions when we were walking to the local shops on the high street that I noticed stereotyping for the first time. On arriving in the shop, the shopkeeper turned around and instead of smiling, froze and turned stern. I wondered why. My father just looked at me, jubilantly, explaining I could have anything on the counter. I couldn't listen to him; I could only look up at the man who looked at my father with such judgement and I wanted to protect my father.

"Are you listening?" he laughed, "I've just said you can have anything. She isn't normally like this," he turned his conversation to the man behind the counter.

The man laughed falsely in return. I didn't understand the word stereotyping at that time, all I knew was that it was the first time in my heart I felt the need to protect my innocent father, who couldn't see, or chose not to see, the man's attitude towards him.

My father dug deep into his shabby jeans pockets, happily counting out the coins for the shopkeeper. In return, whilst taking the money, the man looked at my father as if he was not worthy of walking into his shop at all. I glared at him. He turned to my glare, registered my look, and seemed momentarily uncomfortable at having been caught out.

"Bye," he said, suddenly polite.

"Say bye, then," my father told me, his voice pitching higher in surprised at my obvious ignorance.

"Bye," I waved, not even looking back.

"What's the matter?" my father asked, as we stepped back out into the street.

"I don't like that shop Dad, and I don't like that shopkeeper," I replied, "let's go somewhere else next time."

"Don't be silly," he laughed, "the man's done no wrong; what has he done?" My father seemed puzzled. I didn't tell him why; I couldn't bear the thought of him being upset.

This small town had no men with long hair and also, no black men, but he did teach me about a man called Bob Dylan who had sung about racism.

"That can't happen, Dad," I said. I couldn't imagine people being treated differently – badly – just because of the colour of their skin.

"It does, Michelle, in fact, it has happened and it continues to do so."

He played me his songs of Bob Dylan who told a story about a man called *The Hurricane*. I loved his lessons.

Whenever the weather allowed, we spent hours walking in the countryside, going for long walks across the fields. He would point out birds and animals and explain their behaviours.

One time, he asked my mother if I could stay the night. He woke me in the early hours of the morning to hear the dawn chorus as he took me for the short walk to the woods.

On the day before I went to see my father, my mother would become so hostile and hurtful, telling me again what a worthless person I was. One evening, I couldn't bear to go home. I hid in the shed in my father's back garden. After an hour or so, I heard a car pull up and the sound of police radios. I crept out of the shed and slipped into the shadows at the side of the house, just before the police came outside and searched the shed.

"I know it's strange," I heard a male voice say, "but children are often found in garden sheds."

Once they left, I ran into the field just around the corner. I found the back way in to the sports hall, which kept me out of the wind and squeezed into a small opening. It was now pitch black. I couldn't let anyone see me and I wasn't going home. I realised I couldn't stay there all night, so I walked out onto the main road, trying to think about where I could go. There was nowhere and I was worried about being seen. I decided then that I would go back to my father's and on the way, built up the courage to tell my father about my mother.

Opening the door at my father's house, my mother rushed at me. She slapped me around the face, a look of pure hatred on her face.

"Don't hit her, Denise," my father scolded.

"She always hits me," I cried to him. It was my way in to start speaking about what she was doing wrong. "Please don't let me go home Dad, I want to stay here." I was begging and sobbing hysterically.

"What an earth is going on?" He turned to my mother, a frown forming on his usually calm face.

"Let her stay, Denise," he said. Although he spoke quietly, there was a decisiveness in his voice. "It's OK, come back tomorrow when she's calmed down."

After she'd gone and my father tucked me up in bed like I was a small child again, I finally opened up to him.

"My mother hates me. She calls me names."

He looked confused. "No, no," he said, "That can't be true. Maybe she's just teasing?"

"Please Dad, believe me, I am not going back," I sobbed.

"OK, OK," he soothed, "I promise I will speak to your mother and find out exactly what is going on."

"Thank you."

That night I heard my mother return and she and my father discussing me. She used her exaggeratedly kind voice in answer to the constant questions from my father as to what exactly was going on.

"Of course I love her, Keith, you know I do. She is making it up for attention, we've just had an argument and she wants to live with you."

"It can't be true," he told me the next day. "You've just had an argument."

"You don't believe me," I sobbed.

"I do believe you," he said. "It's difficult for me to have you here. You're too young to understand and what about Neil?"

Neil had come to resent me in a different way from my mother. He simply stopped speaking to me, just as my father's relatives didn't speak to him any more. I was no longer close to Neil and it seemed our relationship ended at the time my mother took me away when I was five. He had wanted to go with her probably as much as I wanted to stay with my father. The separation didn't make any sense at all. It destroyed us.

"But I'll tell you what," my father continued "you can stay here any time you like, you have me now and you're not on your own like you say you are."

It was true, I did have him, but when I was with my mother, I felt alone. She had won again.

At my mother's flat, I could see right into the living room from where I was sitting on the tall stool in the kitchen, all the way over to the furthest wall where the black and white television set was positioned. It had, within seconds, brought life into the silent flat, with its blaring voices and laughter. I remained still in that space, motionless, almost afraid to move. I could see the top of the back of my mum's head; she had been there now for at least five minutes after leaving the kitchen where we'd eaten together, or rather eaten in the same space, without a word. I stared at her, willing her to turn around and look at me. If I told her that I was unhappy, or what made me sad, I knew she would use the information to find even more ways to torment me. Her teasing was acted out in hate; playing with my emotions to the point where she was torturing them at times.

I was learning not to show her what I thought, or how upset I was by how she treated me, because if I did, she would do whatever she was doing even more. I learnt more, every day, how to control my emotions around her so I didn't leak an unconscious mechanism of my mind, revealing to her yet another way to torment me. The name-calling was the worst.

She had left the kitchen this evening with me still in it, switched off the light and didn't even look back. I sat there, legs dangling on a high stool – too high for me to climb down quietly. In that moment, I hesitated and that hesitation gave me a moment of clarity about exactly where I was in this very small family unit. In a way, it provided a moment of sad acceptance, knowing exactly where I stood. I looked over to her again – she looked relaxed now, happy even and warm on her own, without a care in the world, laughing at the programme she was watching. I longed for her to call me into that warmness. I had not experienced that side of her. The two adjacent rooms symbolised where I positioned in my mother's life. It was as though, even though I was stuck here, I just didn't fit and wasn't really welcome.

I imagined, at that moment, how it would be if I were to be snuggled up with her on the sofa, or even on the receiving end of a welcoming smile from her and what it would mean to me. The thought made me feel worse. I was already becoming accustomed to the feelings of loneliness; the realisation of how separate I really was from her intensified that loneliness.

I was permanently afraid and uneasy and always unsure of what I should do next. I wasn't sure what was worse – the feeling of loneliness or the feelings of humiliation when she hurled abuse at me from what seemed to be the middle of nowhere. I was becoming an emotional cripple, but no one could see my wounds. Deep down, I felt like I was a failure. Her words had made me feel inadequate in everything I did and what's more, everything I was. I was nothing...a waste of space. "Nothing" has no right to kindness or respect. "Nothing" has no need for love or understanding, because it's "nothing"...and that's what I was.

My mind was developing ways to foresee every consequence of how my behaviour might trigger a negative outcome from her. I might be hit, or worse, ridiculed or mimicked. Even though I tried to please her, it seemed impossible. Tonight I was left frozen, daring not to speak, or act, or even move.

My mother did have a heart though. She wasn't like this with most other people I saw her with. I often found myself looking up at her face in confusion as she changed into the loving, warm and naturally overly friendly person she was in the many faces of our local community. The only time she seemed happy with me was when I was upset, or when something was going wrong. She seemed, at times, almost like a little girl, craving for attention, like a jealous sibling fighting for first place in the affections of others. She showed nothing but resentment towards me when I got attention, and so I started to hope that others wouldn't give me attention in front of her, especially her friends.

One night, she had a couple of friends around who were encouraging me to come into the room. I sat on the floor in front of my mother, who kicked me in the back when they were talking to each other. I never fought back. I stood up sadly and walked to my room, leaving my mother to explain that's where I liked to sit.

I was still struggling to figure out what the right thing was to do. I seemed to know what was right, but even if I did what was right, it was wrong. It was confusing. I endeavoured to try and please my mother, but nothing worked. I was faced with the painful fact that although I was in her life, I most definitely wasn't in her heart. I was outside it, sitting in another room, a cold room on my own; she kept the warm room for the outside world, just as she'd done tonight.

I stretched off the stool as gently as I could, so that I didn't scrape the legs on the floor as my feet reached the floor. I slowly tiptoed to the kitchen door. When I got to there, I stood for a moment looking in, watching her. I could either go in and join her or disappear to my bedroom and go to bed early so that she would not notice me. That thought made me feel safer, more comforted. In fact, the thought brought me a happier feeling than going in to the family living room. Creeping to the bedroom door, I closed the door behind me and finally felt safe. Tucking myself into bed, I wondered for a moment if she might notice that I wasn't there. I was glad that she hadn't, and didn't, and turned all of my attention to my own little world that I was creating for myself.

6

Chapter 6

Sitting at the back of the flats where I used to live with my mother, on a cold concrete kerb, I was starting to feel cold.

"Put my gloves on," Rebecca insisted, passing me a pair of fingerless gloves. She had just returned with a bottle of cider. Sitting there, a memory of leaving my father when I was only five-years-old flashed, momentarily, through my mind.

I was now thirteen. Rebecca and two other girls began passing the cider around and each took their turn to drink from the bottle.

"Swig it then," she laughed, when it came to me. I sipped a small mouthful of the foul tasting drink.

"I am," I said.

"No," she insisted, "not like that; hold your head back like this." Gulp, gulp, gulp...She was showing me how to drink 'properly' from the bottle of cider to get drunk really quickly. If I was honest with myself, I didn't even want to drink it. I looked at Rebecca for approval and nervously smiled, seeking an indication that I was fitting in with the group. I took the bottle from her and did what she asked.

Glug, glug, glug. I held my head back, taking big swigs, then thrust my head forward again quickly, wiping my mouth from the foul-tasting cider. Everyone laughed, including me. I smiled to myself. I belonged and I felt happy.

Rebecca seemed tough and fearless – I looked to her constantly for approval. She had short hair, spikey on top, a symbol of her confidence and fearless character. She wasn't anything like my mother – in fact, she was the complete opposite; rather than being impossible to please, with Rebecca, anything was OK!

"If we mix this together with lager," she said, "we will get proper drunk." I smiled at her again with my mouth, but not with my heart; my need for her acceptance was greater than the discomfort I felt within myself doing something I really did not want to do. She smiled back wholeheartedly. I felt relieved for a moment, but seconds later, I needed the same reassurance and I smiled again.

"You're too on edge," Rebecca said to me, in a sisterly way. "Get some of this down you, it will make you feel better."

It was a seal of acceptance, completed by her sitting next to me and giving me a big bear hug and patting me on the back when I spluttered after another huge swig from the bottle.

I wasn't too sure, at first, about getting proper drunk, but minutes later, I started to feel a sense of freedom – a sense that nothing mattered and we began to roam the streets together.

Our friendship lasted two years, to when I was fifteen years old. I often hid behind Rebecca's bold personality, hoping that no one would notice that mine wasn't actually developed.

My mum's mimicking hadn't stopped and the outbursts of physical violence had begun to get worse.

"Get out of the fucking way," she would snarl as she passed me in the small, narrow kitchen of our home.

In spite of my friendship with Rebecca, inside I still felt pathetic and weak. I seemed to make friends quickly enough, despite being so unsure of myself. I also had an inner strength, resilience and endurance, which I didn't see at the time. It always took me a couple of days to open up to new friends and start speaking, but once I got over the initial fear, I was fine around people, as long as I didn't speak about myself. I often tried to be brash to cover up my lack of confidence.

My father also shifted into the background of my life again and I spent most of my free time with my friends.

Now that I was older, I had also started to care for my disabled younger brother again. Learning to put other people before myself was a great quality I was forming. I did not know, however, how to make my own decisions and please myself, always putting my own problems to the back shelf in my life. My main concern was still analysing my mother and trying to understand how I might please her. Having long given up trying to work out all of the inconsistencies, I came to the conclusion that if I mirrored her behaviour, then I had to get it right. I also started to mirror the behaviour of others around me, often going along with them, even if I didn't agree with what they were doing, because I simply had no idea how to be myself. I copied my friends, even though they let me know how much it annoyed them sometimes, but I knew was intelligent in other ways. I was in most top sets at school for Maths and English, being able to pick up information and understand those things quite easily.

My mother had started to say, 'Who do you think you are?' when I came in from being with my friends. I knew she sensed my growing independence, but I didn't understand the anger and aggression in this new question. The only time I could vaguely remember upsetting her for a good reason was dropping a whole glass bottle of milk on the doorstep. It was the only time I could think of that, in some way, justified the smacking around my head and name-calling.

For some reason, the 'Who do you think you are?' question, repeated again and again, brought all of my fears and doubts to a crescendo. Who *was* I? Who *did* I think I was? A new set of feelings, that I now know to be depression, had set in. It was crushing me in ways I wasn't fully aware of and my depressed state told me there was no hope for my future. I had begun to feel loneliness to its extreme. *I was not worth being loved*, I told myself and my thinking pattern mirrored my mother's words. *Nothing would make me happier than if I didn't wake up one day.* And there it was, the answer, as if the answer to all my prayers, had arrived. I would take all my brother's tablets and not wake up in the morning. I had not felt happier for a long time – I had found a resolution to all my problems, which were going to come to an end. The emotional pain I was in was going to stop and I had found hope in an obscure way.

I waited one evening until my mother had gone to bed and I sneaked out of my bedroom, tip toeing downstairs to the kitchen. The house was as quiet as always – I felt like an uncomfortable stranger in someone else's house. I was on edge and my ears were on hyper vigilance as I reached up to the kitchen cupboard for the many bottles of tablets belonging to my younger brother. There were at least ten bottles there of different sorts. I was strangely happy and relieved, not sad, as I'd imagined most people would be, about committing suicide. I didn't cry like I normally would when my mother called me names. I didn't feel like I was losing anything, only a life of name-calling, loneliness and pain. In fact, I felt empowered, probably for the first time in a long time, as if I had gained a final answer. As I lined up the tablets, I counted them – I wasn't leaving it to chance. I took a couple out of each bottle, ensuring he still had plenty of what he needed, but I was determined to take as many as I could. I couldn't risk the chance of waking up in the morning. This was my only way out.

The taste was awful and even though they were coated with plastic they were hard to swallow. I took at least forty. I could have taken more if it wasn't for the fact I had started to heave whilst I was still taking them. I couldn't risk being sick. I took myself upstairs and slowly I lay down in my bed so I didn't disturb my stomach and throw them all back up. I lay there, looking out my bedroom window for the last time and I smiled to myself. There was no more harm that could be done to me. No more lies would I have to endure about me to other people and it no longer mattered if no one heard me or even believed me. *Go to sleep,* I said to myself, calmly and peacefully, *it will all be over soon.*

When I opened my eyes in the morning, the first thing I felt was a crashing disappointment. It had not worked. I had survived somehow, even though I had taken so many tablets. When I woke, there was no one in the house. My mother had gone out and I was glad, because I felt so ill and knew I wouldn't have coped well, facing the disappointment that I hadn't escaped her. I heard a strange buzzing noise in my head. It went louder and quieter like a hoover and I worried about the noise. It was constant. What had I done? A sickening realisation crashed over me now, that I might have damaged my body. The door bell rang. I didn't want to answer it, but I did anyway and standing there, strong and as brash as ever, was my aunt.

"Are you listening to me?" she said abruptly, but kindly, as I stood at the door just staring at her, while she gave me a message to pass on to my mum.

"I just feel dizzy," I explained.

"You're not pregnant are you?"

I hadn't even started having boyfriends, but I couldn't tell her the truth.

"I can hear something in my brain," I told her. "I think I'm ill."

"Do you think you are pregnant?" she asked again. I said nothing.

"You think you are, don't you?" The very next day, I was carted off to the doctor's, listening to my aunt telling him to put me on the pill.

"I don't need them," I told the doctor, but I was just relieved that the noise in my head had gone – I had probably had a lucky escape.

"Next time, don't bloody waste my time," my aunt snapped as we left the doctor's.

So, as my only escape from the constant despair, meeting my friends on the street with a bottle of cider and a can of lager was so much better than being at home. When I eventually did get in at night, I headed for the toilet. That night, I woke her. She followed me to the bathroom, screaming at me.

"You're drunk, you little bitch," she said, as she smelt my breath before I started to heave. I began to vomit.

She started hitting me, still screeching.

"You're good for nothing... I told you you were nothing... look at you... wait till I tell your Dad what you've become."

I didn't care. I smiled inwardly to myself, because the alcohol had numbed the effects of the hitting; her words just bounced off me and for the first time, I felt nothing of the effects of her abuse. I was drunk and I felt like I had won a small battle by not feeling any pain and by not caring. A rebellious voice spoke in my head, *if she is going to tell everyone I'm bad, I might as well be bad.* Perhaps it was a good thing I hadn't died, after all.

MICHELLE NICHOLSON

Chapter 7

"I'm going to live at my Dad's at the weekends," I told her defiantly, a few weeks later. She was following me towards the door, shouting. I answered her back, no longer caring about the consequences.

"Don't you answer me back, you good for nothing…"

It was useless – her words had begun to lose their power and authority over me. I no longer cared what anyone thought of me, especially *her*, my mother. She had already driven me to the bottom of a pit and there was no going any lower. I was also driven by a need to belong to my father again, following the freedom gained from adolescence. Rebecca and I had begun to visit my Dad, prompted by her curiosity about where I came from. I was pretending, not only to her, but also to myself, that was where I belonged; in reality, I didn't really know. I still longed for family life and I was now going to get my father back. For once, I was taking the decision into my own hands. Standing at the door, I put on my coat and turned to leave.

My mother roared, "No, you are not going out, get your coat off and get back in this house!"

"Yes, I am," I replied, disregarding her words completely, still walking through the door.

"He doesn't want you," she spat, a look of cruel triumph in her eyes.

"Yes, he does, Mum, I've already asked him and I'm going to stay this weekend."

This battle was over.

I no longer had any respect for her. I yearned no longer for her love at that moment. She had humiliated me to my limit and left me with the feeling that I had nothing left. I picked up my bag and left the house like an empty vessel, hoping that I would fill it with something from my father.

My mother had become ill when we had first moved into a new house, a year or so before. Looking back now, she had probably been ill for most of my life. She would say strange things about persecution and wouldn't even go outside to empty the bin, sometimes. It was during that time she complained that people were talking about her, accusing her of leaving my disabled brother and me to go to work. It was also at that time she had taken us both to my father's to look after us. Living in a town she didn't grow up in must have also been isolating for her. She had moved from Liverpool to Bridlington to be with my father. By the time I had moved to the secondary school, she started to cover the windows with sheets and I wasn't allowed to put the TV on.

'Ssshhh', she told me one day, 'they're watching us'. It scared me. *Who might be watching us?* I wondered.

'The government is watching us,' she reiterated her fears another day, as I went to put the TV on again. The mirrors were also covered, along with the windows.

'They're after us,' she'd say, out of the blue, a strange look on her face and in her eyes.

I was scared, not because I believed her, but because of how she was acting and looking. It occurred to me something was seriously wrong. I was a child and the only other person in the house – I was incapable of diagnosing what was wrong, or figuring out how to help her. I could not rationalise with her. Eventually, I turned to my father for help.

Coming home from school one day, I saw the social services woman leading my Mum out of the house and forcing her into a car.

"Is there anywhere you can stay, Michelle?" the blonde lady shouted, in the middle of a scuffle with my mother.

"Yes, of course, I'll stay with my father," I replied. She looked relieved.

"Your Mum's ill, Michelle," she explained, still tackling my mother.

After several electric shock treatments and after listening to my Mum complain that she was being abused in the local mental health unit, by being held down to take her medication and other accusations of unprofessional behaviour, she was allowed to come home. She was never the same person, when she came out, as she was when she went in.

It was, however, at the same time my mum became ill, that she stopped calling me names and hitting me, for a time. It occurred to me that I had an explanation for my years of mental, emotional and physical beatings. I felt helpless, watching her as she sat staring into space. I vowed to get her better – now that I knew the root of her behaviours towards me, I once again had hope of a real relationship between us. I made sure she ate and I even bathed her. Once, I made a stance about her medication and stopped her from going to the doctors.

"She is not going," I argued with Aunty Anne, trying to protect my mother. I was watching her turn into an empty shell and I blamed vast numbers of pills.

That was when my Aunty Anne had to sit me down and tell me what was wrong with my mother.

"Michelle, you can't make her better on your own. She needs the medication to get better. She cannot live normally without it. She is diagnosed with schizophrenia. It's a serious mental illness. You can't see it, though, Michelle, like a broken leg. She has a broken mind, but she's ill all the same."

As soon as my mother became better again and was used to the medication, she started to treat me in the same cruel way. I was glad I'd made the link with my father for an escape.

In a strange way, it had helped that he had walked in one day when she was in the middle of an attack on me, something no one had witnessed before and I was crying pathetically, like a baby.

"What the hell is going on?" he cried. "No, Denise, you can't do that, can't you see she's on the verge of an emotional breakdown."

I had revelled in my friends' acceptance so much, I even changed my look to be like them and painted on big black eyeliner, copying my friend Rebecca and went to the extreme of wearing black lipstick just like her, too. When I walked into my father's house with it on, he would often be cooking tea and ask, 'What have you got on your lips?' It didn't feel like he was judging or criticising me, more that he was just curious. The weekends staying with my father were good, in the sense that I felt safe again. I belonged and I was treated like a human being.

My older brother Neil, however, wasn't as pleased about my stay and acted as though I was intruding on his life. He still lived with my father and made it obvious I was not welcome. He often called me awful names, more bullying than teenage arguing. When he swore at me and shunned me, it made me feel as helpless as I was with my mother. I wasn't able to brush awful comments off, or argue back with him like a normal teenager would. Instead I acted more like a child, left with a sense of inability to defend myself and unable to flip his comments back. They pierced and crippled me nearly as much as my mother's comments had. I had learnt to become helpless.

'Leave her alone', my father would say to Neil, stepping in to defend me, when I obviously couldn't. He also had a good side to him, but unlike my mother, who showed only her good side to other people, he occasionally showed me that good side, too. I had become too defensive with him and often lost out on those moments, because I was not prepared for them. I did ask myself at times, *why does he hate me? Is it because I went to live with my mother and he didn't? What was it like for him to lose a mother who loved him?* Although this tarnished my stay a little, it didn't take away the positive relationship I had with my Dad.

I asked my dad if I could move in permanently, but he said it wouldn't be fair on my mother and that she relied on me, not out of choice. Perhaps he knew that she might just need me again. He never fully understood the extent of the mind games and abuse I suffered when I went home, no matter how hard I attempted to explain.

My mother had even asked a friend to intervene at one point, in an attempt to prevent me from staying at my fathers. My mother was trying to use my father's small time drug use to disallow my visits.

Rebecca and the crowd began to venture further away from our neighbourhood and closer to the town centre.

"Who's going in to the off licence tonight?" Rebecca asked. No one answered.

"Michelle, you go!" Rebecca insisted, knowing that she always got refused. For some reason the shopkeepers didn't always ask my age. I had recently had my hair cut into an older, more sophisticated style and had started to care about my image. I had come to love clothes and that became a part of my personality – I had finally started to develop and show who I was. I had dressed in second hand, dowdy clothes growing up. Clothes had given me a new found confidence – something on which to build a personality.

"OK," I said, apprehensively. I was happy to be needed and wanted the alcohol as much as them.

"But don't look around the shop too much, you need to act older and confident."

One of my few lessons in being confident, ironically, was needed to get alcohol for my friends. I listened and did everything she advised. I took a deep breath. The shop door bell pinged as I walked in. The shopkeeper looked at me momentarily and I took Rebecca's advice about confidence. I looked her straight in the face, instead of holding my head down and wishing she wasn't looking at me. Then, I went straight to the cheapest bottles of cider and lager. I took the cider to the desk and put the bottle on the counter, as confidently as I could. The shopkeeper looked confused for a split second. I started speaking casually about the weather, holding her gaze.

"Thank you, have a good evening." I smiled at her, straight in the eyes and picked up the bag.

Still looking confused, she smiled back at me; a young girl acting like a thirty-year-old. I was a fast learner.

That evening, my life was about to change. We all walked to a quiet spot off the main road and opened our bottles of cider. Not long after, some other kids approached.

"What are you doing here?" one of the boys asked.

"We're just hanging out," I replied, being friendly.

Some of my friends didn't look too happy.

"Come on, Michelle, don't talk to them. We're going."

At exactly that point, I felt something come over me instinctively. It told me that if I went with these people my life would change forever. I couldn't explain it and didn't try to; everyone would have thought I was mad. I knew I couldn't live my life wandering the streets every night forever and that something would have to change at some point. When these new kids invited me back to their house out of the cold, I was intrigued.

I said, yes, and didn't even know why. Spending the next couple of nights with these new friends, I eventually met Mathew, who was a year older than me in my school.

A year later, I found myself at the local chemist, buying a pregnancy test.

"I hope that's not for you," a stern looking woman said from across the counter. I didn't need the pregnancy test to know I was pregnant. I felt different inside.

Mathew was my first proper boyfriend. I had never felt happier in my life than when I looked at the pregnancy test that day. That happiness didn't end, even though, shortly after I told Mathew I was pregnant, our relationship ended. I was fifteen and no one could take this little being away from me. I had tried all this time to belong and here I was, blessed with something so special.

"Mum," I said, when I got home. She had started to become ill again. I sat beside her on the bed; she hadn't got up for weeks and I was now caring for again. She looked at me and acknowledged what I said without judging me, for the first time.

"I'm going to get better," she said, "so I can help you."

And that's what she did. It seemed the coming birth of my daughter was not only bringing me hope, she was bringing hope to us all. *Perhaps life was going to change, after all,* I smiled to myself. Although, not in the way I had imagined. It was better than I had imagined. I was going to have a baby. I was pregnant at fifteen and I was as happy as I could be.

Chapter 8

I looked down at my perfect baby girl as I lay in the hospital bed – she was the most beautiful thing I'd ever seen in my whole life – she relied on me for her every need – I was her mother! As I held her for the first time, I felt the powerful connection of the mother and daughter bond. I had to protect this little creature – she was dependent upon me for everything. I made a promise there and then that she was never going to have a life like mine. I was going to make her the most confident person and she would never go without love. In fact, I was going to give her the *perfect* life.

It was clear that my mother also loved my daughter and she helped out for the first couple of months, although I was keen to do the most of the duties. Not long after, however, her behaviour towards me deteriorated again and she started to insult me and shove me when she walked past. Even knowing about her mental health condition, I was as heartbroken, realising that she just did not want to accept me.

I was, up until that point, a happy and content mother, feelings which had started to develop when I pregnant.

"You're glowing," everyone would comment when they passed me with my daughter.

Maybe that was the cause of my mother's deterioration into ill health again – she couldn't bear to see me happy and confident.

One day, Mum barged into my room, in what seemed to be a jealous outburst, whilst I was feeding my daughter.

"Who do you think you are?" she yelled, striking me over and over. Falling backwards onto my small sofa in the room, I knew I could never let her hit me again.

I trembled as I stood up to her, "Don't hit me," I said. "You could have hurt my daughter."

"Don't be stupid," she replied, "I would never hurt your daughter." She tried to laugh it off, but her face told me she knew that she had crossed the line and looked worried about the consequences if I told anyone.

Then, completely out of the blue one day, I returned home to find a locked door, with no answer to my knocking. I had never been given a key.

Standing outside, the locked door with my daughter in her pram, I was almost relieved, in spite of my shock – I felt that this was the start of a new era for me.

I never lived with my mother again, from that day to this and she never again hit me. That's not to say, however, that she didn't hurt me again.

Later that same day, I stood outside my father's door, taking a deep breath, hoping my brother Neil would now accept me, as I knew my father would.

"Can I live here, Dad," I asked nervously, knowing I didn't have anywhere to go.

"Of course," he said and at last, I was home. This time, however, no longer in the role of the young rebel, but of a young teenage mother who loved her daughter.

It was three whole years of bliss and he was reluctant to let me go because of it. I had found a flat to mark my independence and to start a life with a boyfriend I had been in a relationship with for two years. I felt as though we had a happy future together. Looking back, I should never have left.

"You don't have to go," my dad pleaded, and I knew he was hurt. "You can stay here."

"I'll be OK, Dad." I hugged him. "Neil doesn't want me here and we both know it. I'll come and stay on weekends."

If it weren't for the fact that my brother had made it difficult for me to live there, I would have probably remained there for a little while longer. I did, however, want to prove my independence as a young mother and I signed up for college, which now meant that I had a plan to work towards for a positive future for my daughter and me. The college had a crèche and I felt happy that I had begun to carve a future for us both. My father was proud of me and he kissed me on my cheek as I left.

Not long after we moved in together, I had to tell my boyfriend to leave. Our relationship had lasted three years, most of it whilst living with my father, but it turned bad when we moved in together. We had made long term plans, but he didn't accept my daughter the way I'd believed he had. I discovered my daughter was on the edge, a close call of abuse by him. Although she wasn't hurt, I was left devastated by it – I felt that because I'd been naïve and believed he had cared for her, I'd failed to properly protect her. It was a hard lesson – even though I had caught it before anything happened, for the mother who had promised the perfect life to her daughter, I was destroyed.

Getting him out of my flat, however, was easy. I called the police – I wanted justice for my daughter.

"Just be thankful you have stopped it before it started," the policewoman comforted me. I was inconsolable that he was not to face justice. It was the most vulnerable time I had ever faced in my life up to then and as far as I was concerned, I was a failure. I was emotionally crushed that the only thing I wanted to do right in my life had gone wrong. My conscience punished me far too harshly – even though I had saved her – I was a complete mess.

My father was the only person to continue to help me and stop me from punishing myself. I stayed again with him for weekends and odd days. I sought counselling and needed the closeness of my father for comfort, while I punished myself with my thoughts, just as my mother had done with her words.

It was not long after that time that I met Jane. She was a little older than me (although I was never really sure how much older) and lived near my father. I first met her when I was walking past her house with my friend Vanessa, one summer.

There was an obvious party going on in her house, with loud music booming and several men drinking and laughing in the garden.

"Oi, you!" she shouted across to us both. "Come to my party."

"Keep walking," Vanessa said, not even looking up. Vanessa was focused and had a far stronger mind than me and had been supportive to me for some time. She reminded me constantly that what almost happened with my daughter was not my fault, and that I needed to stop blaming myself.

"You have an air of innocence," Vanessa told me on another occasion. "It's easy for people to tap into your need for acceptance – you allow people to take advantage of you. You need to be stronger."

She tried to stick some of my broken parts together and give me some of her wisdom. She watched my crushed girl's self-esteem as a young man picked me up and threw me down as he pleased. Love was all I needed, but who could love me in such a mess?

It wasn't easy to avoid Jane, I had to pass her house to get into town or anywhere I usually went. Vanessa had warned me not to get involved with her, and I was taking that advice seriously. When I did have to pass her house, I tried not to look up, or to give her any encouragement to engage with me.

"Hey, you," she shouted over one day, as I walked on the opposite side of the road. "What's up with you? Don't you like the look of me or something?" I was stunned and didn't know how to answer. She obviously couldn't take the hint that I didn't want to know her.

"No, of course not," I explained myself to her, smiling nervously.

"OK!" she said, laughing "Don't look so scared then. If that's true you will come into my house and have a coffee."

And that's how I met her properly for the first time. She had set the tune for a strange relationship that, to me, had a very clear imbalance of power from the start. It could not really be called a friendship – I was afraid of her, always trying to make sure I said and did the right thing. She, on the other hand, seemed to enjoy the power she had over me. She was aggressive by nature, similar to my mother and I was more afraid of Jane than I was of my mother or my brother. I didn't want to be on the end of her wrath, as other people were. She had a jealous streak and spoke of her resentment for other women who had, she seemed to believe, taken some of her men from her. Jane had had a lot of boyfriends, sometimes more than one at a time.

"The police come to my house," she boasted one day. She showed me her room – there was a whip in it. I hid my shock, but I was beginning to think she was more than a little weird. Her other friends, most of them men, just went along with her ways as though they were normal.

My father's friend, Mickey, also warned me off her. He was standing watching one night and saw one of her boyfriends spying on her house, watching the coming and going of several men. Mickey warned me to stay away from her, telling me, "I just don't like her, she has too many men coming and going from her house, something's not right."

It wasn't just Vanessa and Mickey who held those views, it seemed. One evening, when I was returning from the shop to my father's, a man from the local community told me, "Stay away from Jane." Although I had never spoken to him, he seemed to care about my wellbeing. It was definitely a warning. The tone was alarming. I spoke to Jane about it next time I saw her.

"Someone's told me to stay away from you, too!" she spat, immaturely. Why would anyone tell her to stay away from me? I didn't really do anything, other than bring my daughter up with the help of my father. *Who was she and what was I getting into?* I did however, continue to maintain contact with her – that was the choice I made and it was the worst choice of my life.

One evening, I was passing her house. She looked angry.

"Come to Driffield with me," she said, "my boyfriend has caught me kissing Greg outside my house, my son's father, and I want to speak to him."

It was another ridiculous choice I made, but my choice all the same.

"How are we going to get there?"

"Do you want to help or not?"

I felt shamed by her covert accusation and my conscience about that overwhelmed my good common sense. On the way, she told me her plan. She was going to tell the boyfriend, whom she had betrayed, that she was pregnant. As we neared the house, a lovely woman, who seemed distraught to see Jane and hear her news, greeted us.

"I hate his mother," Jane had said on the way, in the car. "I don't know who she thinks she is, she thinks the sun shines out of her son's arse. I am going to give her something to think about."

The boy's mother and I sat in the living room whilst Jane and the boy argued for a couple of minutes. I looked down at the woman's white carpet, thinking this perfect house had been contaminated with Jane and her news. He mother sat next to me, looking shocked. Jane cared nothing for the boy's mother. She had walked into her house disrespecting not only her son, but also her.

"My shoes," I said, repeatedly. The older woman wasn't listening. "I need to take them off. Where shall I put them?"

"I don't care about the carpet," she said, sadly. She looked at me for hope. "Is she really pregnant, Michelle? I can cope with someone being pregnant. but I don't know what he sees in her and I'm scared for my son."

I felt afraid too, knowing the damage I was being implicated in.

"She's not pregnant." I looked to her. "Please don't tell her I told you, she scares me."

"I promise you, Michelle, I won't say anything."

The woman hugged me and looked so relieved.

"Thank you, thank you, thank you."

"Why are you her friend?" she asked, confused.

"I don't know," I replied, truthfully.

"You must be able to get better friends than her; you're lovely."

I had lots of friends and none of them were like Jane. At the worst, I felt weak and pathetic around her. She would insist I hadn't treated her right by not going around all the time and I tried to please her by giving her a beauty treatment to make up for it. I didn't want to be here tonight, but it was too late, I'd already agreed to come.

The woman got her strength back and took control of her house. Jane was angry when she was ordered to leave.

"Thank you," his mother mouthed to me, as we left the house. We were now stranded about fifteen miles from home.

On the dark road of the estate, a man was walking his dog. Jane shouted out to him.

"Hey you," she said, rudely, "we're stranded." The man looked sympathetic. He and Jane began talking quietly. I walked behind them and realised she was flirting with the older man. *When was this night going to end?* I just wanted to be at home with my father.

He led us to his home and invited us in.

"Can I use your phone?" I asked.

He and Jane continued into the living room, chatting and laughing.

"Mum," I gasped quickly, as soon as she answered the phone. "I need you to get a message to Dad, I am stranded and have no…."

Before I could finish the sentence, my mother shouted, "Tough" and I was left listening to the high pitch of the phone telling me the line was dead. I really was stranded.

"What are you phoning your Mum for?" Jane scoffed.

I went upstairs to use the toilet and was shocked when I looked through an open bedroom door to see Jane going through the owner's belongings, as he sat downstairs watching the TV.

"What are you doing?" I asked her.

"What does it fucking look like I'm doing?" she spat.

I went downstairs and waited in the kitchen to leave. The man was in the living room, trusting Jane in his house.

"What's up with you," she sneered, when she re-appeared

downstairs. She could sense I was judging her and she clearly didn't like my attitude. She was also angry she had lost her boyfriend. I hadn't even noticed the purse on the counter, but Jane spotted it as soon as she came into the kitchen.

"Get that purse," she demanded, even though it was within her reach. I looked, shocked. "Get it," she demanded.

I was afraid and picked up the purse and handed it to her. She hid it down her trousers.

She sneered at me again. "What's wrong with you, you think you're too good? Well, you just stole that purse, so you're a thief."

As soon as I got into my father's house, I told him what had happened. He walked me right over to Mickey's for advice. There was nothing I would hide from him. He looked disappointed for me and I promised to him that I would stay away from Jane from then on. Six months later, I was in court for theft. I had only handed the purse from the kitchen top to her. She could have picked it up herself, but I later suspected she had done it that way specifically to implicate me. A long list of Jane's previous convictions was read out in court. It was my first offence.

My father sensed my feelings of shame and failure. My mother exacerbated them by informing the whole of the local community of the criminal act I had committed.

"Ignore your mother," my father tried to comfort me, witnessing my clear discomfort in facing the consequences of my previous actions. I loved him for his unconditional love and his unfailing protection, despite my young mistakes.

Chapter 9

"You're gullible," Jo said gently. She was a good friend I'd made in college and she'd listened to me recount another situation that I'd hoped would bring me happiness. She could easily see the disappointment I felt inside, in my expression.

"Don't believe everything everyone tells you," she said, lightly. I sighed to myself deeply, looking down in shame at my college folder in my lap. I picked it up and held it tightly, knowing it represented a potential future for my daughter and me.

I had become immersed in an inner battle with an over exaggerated conscience telling me, every day, that I was worthless. I needed and craved positive feedback from others, to the extent that it had made me vulnerable to social peers. Jo sensed my sadness. She gave me a big, sisterly bear hug and kissed me on my forehead, leaving a bright red lipstick mark. I forced a smile, comforted by her obvious and genuine hand of friendship. Jo was a caring young woman who sensed my neediness and gave me the reassurance I needed through her friendship. It was a friendship that was to endure the test of time.

For now, it had kept me away from the bad influences of my past. I hadn't seen, or been in contact with Jane for more than two years – if I did bump into her, I always had the excuse of college and my daughter to avoid having to interact with her.

"My father is killing himself," I confided in Jo one day, at her flat in the centre of town. I'd begun to have concerns about his health and his increased intake of drugs, since he had recently made some new acquaintances, in early 1993. It was obvious not only to me, but to others around him, that these people were not as desirable as his older, loyal friends. Jo looked at me with concern as I poured out my heart to her that morning.

"I'm afraid that the drugs are going to go too far and I'm going to lose him." I told her.

One of those new acquaintances, a man called Lewis, wasn't like the rest of my father's friends. It was commonly believed that, in the guise of a friend, he gave drugs to the vulnerable people he befriended, and they all went on to become his customers, becoming trapped because of their new addictions. He was classed as *low life,* even by the community my father lived in. It was certainly true that it was only after Lewis came into my father's life that my father began to turn to harder drugs.

He had begun to seem confused at times – it was this confusion that revealed to me that he was using harder drugs.

At my coaxing, he agreed to attend drug counselling and I attended regularly with him, for support. I had never known him to be as vulnerable as he had now become. He was forty-six years old, becoming lost in a phase of regretting his past and all of his lost opportunities. He also felt like he'd failed at bringing me up – yet, as far as I was concerned – he had been the best father.

I understood that sense of failure, though, I'd battled with it most of my life. Now, I was truly afraid. My father had been my rock, my protector, the one person who always understood when I battled the inner feelings of failure and inadequacy. Without his support and guidance, I was terrified of dealing with those feelings alone.

I was losing him at the time I needed him most and that loss began in the form of Lewis, the man who, it was commonly believed, preyed on local drug users to feed his own habit.

"I don't like him," I told my Dad, sensing that he was getting out of his depth, in a similar way to how I'd felt I'd been overpowered by Jane's will just a couple of months earlier.

He was called to attend a course at the local job centre, in an attempt to engage him and others like him to return to the job market. Every evening, he would return from the course with paper work in the pocket of his worn, purple, velvet jacket and put it in the drawer in his living room cabinet, ready for the next day. I missed him on the days he was away; it wasn't like him to be away and we had got accustomed to his daily presence. Always in awe of my father, I hung onto every word he spoke and without him knowing, one day, I pulled out his work to read it, almost like a parent eager to know of the progress of a child in school. My father was an intelligent man. Standing at the cabinet, I read his words. There was a list of questions relating to work, identifying barriers to employment. One particular question stood out to me: 'Are you proud of what you have achieved in life?' I recognised my father's handwriting, the neat and artistic form he was taught in the 50s. It read, 'I am ashamed that I have achieved nothing in my life at all and there is very little I have done with my life. I feel like I have failed and the only thing I can be proud of is my children.'

My heart jolted. The realisation that my perfect father, who was so wise and peaceful, had regrets came as a painful revelation to me. My empathy with him seemed intensified by those feelings of failure of my own. There was nothing more I wanted, at that point, than to comfort him and take those feelings away. I felt like a parent who had read their child's homework and discovered the child's inner pain.

"I am so proud of you," I told him, completely out of the blue one day. He looked up at me, confused, unaware that I had read his homework. I was now becoming his parent. I was the parent of not only him, but also my mother, who started to rely on me more and more, as she helplessly struggled with her mental health condition.

"You are the perfect parent," I continued. I wasn't lying. He was everything a parent should have been. A protector. A teacher. A comforter. He had always been there for me. And now, even though I needed him, he needed me more.

As well as the increased uptake in his substance misuse, my father had also begun to drink. One day, I found both of my parents waiting for me, in my flat, when I got in. My father was the worse for wear and had come to see me, to share his feelings of regret and disappointment with his life. I was honoured, in a sad sort of way.

"Are you OK, Dad?" I asked, watching a once proud, wise man crying like a lost boy, recounting his failings and his regrets.

"I don't think the drinking is helping you at all, Dad," I told him on another day, as he repeated the same scenario again and again. He was always more regretful, more disappointed with himself and his life, after he had been drinking. I suggested that perhaps he should cut down.

I lived with my daughter and she was the best thing that had ever happened to me. I loved her. But I still carried the feeling of loneliness in my heart from my childhood, and my thoughts told me every day that I was a failure, even though I was studying at college and achieving, just like all my other peers around me.

I had always sought out my father for help and one day, he took me to a counselling session and sat in the waiting room with a can of lager in his hand, trying to help me, even though he was disappearing into his own void.

In the counselling room, I struggled to speak. A kind man sat in silence, waiting for me to speak. I was wracked with an insurmountable load of guilt over the failed relationship that had come so close to harming my daughter and could not face my over-exaggerated conscience – the feeling of being responsible for and failing at, everything. I had failed, just like my mother had said I would, all those years ago. I didn't hear her voice any more, I only heard my own. That inner voice had not gone away and over the years had worsened, focusing on things that had not worked out and never even noticing the things I had achieved.

My father and I were both becoming lost at the same time.

I realised my father's drinking was starting to cause serious problems when my mother turned to me for help.

"Your Dad has been around here asking for money," she complained one day.

"Well, don't give it to him, then."

My visits to my mother had become more regular once my college course finished and I was a qualified beauty therapist in the May of 1993. That apparently normal young girl, who took on everyone's problems, was actually becoming less capable of coping with everything; in fact, I voiced my concerns to my mother about bearing her load.

Her mental health issues put her in the mind-set in which everything revolved around her. She continued to rely on me for everything and I felt compelled to visit her more, to give her company and offer what support I could.

"He's taken my purse," she accused one day, when I arrived at her house after taking my daughter to school. I walked around to my fathers to get it back for her.

"Do you have Mum's purse?" I was always on my father's side, but today wasn't about sides; I was merely performing my duty in my new role as a parent of two siblings.

"Thank you, I said calmly, as he handed it over. I returned it to my mother and told her she would have to start solving her own problems. If she was not happy with Dad, then she should not let him in.

A couple of days later, Mum gloated.

"Your Dad's not happy with you," she laughed.

She changed, without warning, from the role of the helpless mother to the bitter, lonely, jealous woman now smiling vindictively before me. I felt a huge pain in my heart. It was the first time there had been any rift in my relationship with my father. We had never argued or rowed in our life. He was my best friend and remained so, even though he was temporarily not himself.

"That's it," I told her. "You can sort out your own problems from now on." She laughed. It had made her day.

Once again, I was struggling to cope with everything. In a desperate cry for help, I had swallowed too many paracetamol tablets. I wanted someone, somewhere to recognise how difficult my life had become. Without my dad to turn to, I was lost.

A week later, I bumped into Jane again. She pulled up in a strange looking, loud car and shouted over to me at my weakest moment.

"Where have you been?" she sneered at me, annoyed. "You think you're too good for me, don't you?"

"No," I replied, but I knew she was *no* good for me.

"Then where have you been?" she demanded.

I was glad to have an excuse at the forefront of my mind. I should have just told her that I was looking after my mother. Instead, I told her I was not coping, hoping that she might understand that I didn't want to see her – I had too much else to deal with in my life. I'd managed to avoid her now for almost three years, when I did see her, I always had the excuse of going to college. Even after all this time, she intimidated me.

"What do you mean," she squealed, making me feel inferior and that I had to explain myself.

That's exactly what I did.

"I took a heap of pills," I told her.

She looked annoyed and impatient – I knew she was dismissing my words as attention seeking. I was already fragmented and was trying to build myself up; I really didn't need Jane putting me down and making me doubt myself further.

"That's stupid," she snapped, "you didn't want to take your life, or you would have been dead." She was right and she was cold.

"Why did you do it?" she demanded in the street, not allowing me any sort of privacy or dignity.

"I'm lonely," I told her.

"I'm going round to see Mark," she announced. "Why don't you come with me?"

I didn't want to and just stood looking at her.

"You just told me you're fucking lonely," she snapped, angrily, "just come to the house." She eased up a little and said she'd drop me off in a bit. I agreed, reluctantly, and her face softened.

Even though I wasn't keen to be forced to be in Jane's company, I was glad I would see Mark, he was warm, thoughtful and kind. I had passed the time of day with him for the last couple of years, especially when I lived in the flat. At that time, he had lived on the same street; he always seemed to be a sensitive kind of guy.

Jane was eager to offload as soon as I got in her car.

"I've given Mark gonorrhoea and both Greg and Mark are going to go mad ... I got it off this guy I met the other week ... you're not fucking listening are you? I've just listened to you, well, now it's time for you to listen to me."

I wasn't listening. Her problems didn't seem all that serious and were, as far as I could see, all of her own making. It seemed that she just wanted someone to confide in, or rather, offload onto.

When we arrived at Mark's house, there was another man there that I didn't know. He seemed a bit odd. His name was Scott. He seemed to me to be overly controlled and intense. I felt instantly uncomfortable in his presence. Mark, on the other hand, gave off the same aura as my father. Deep down, I thought him to be as trustworthy as my father.

Just as we were leaving, Mark called us back half-heartedly from the opened living room window.

"Scott likes you and wants to meet up with you," he told me, referring to the man in his living room who had stared at me intensely. "What shall I tell him?" he shrugged, looking embarrassed.

"Tell him I'm busy." I was on my way to completing a final assessment at college before the end of term. I was almost in the car when the man, himself, shouted out of the window.

"What are you doing tomorrow?"

"I'm going to my mum's."

Meaning I was busy. He was persistent.

"Can I see you there?"

Pathetically, I gave him the address. Where the hell was my ability to say *no?*

When the knock came to my mother's door the next day, I hid in the back room.

"I know who it is," I said to my mother, "tell him I'm not here."

"I'm not bloody lying for you."

Maybe she had every right to refuse, but she would have made it a lot easier on me that day, knowing I had not one ounce of assertiveness.

"I'm sorry, I can't let you in," I told him, when I answered the door. "I'm on my way to college to pick my certificates up and then I'm going to see my cousin."

"I'll give you a lift." He wouldn't get the message and remained standing at the door. I sighed, anything to make him go. Walking to his car, he ducked, which I thought was strange behaviour.

"I'm a Jehovah's Witness," he explained. "I can't let those people across the road see me."

I couldn't wait to get away from this peculiar man.

When he parked outside the college, I thanked him for the lift and attempted to end our brief time together, opening the door quickly to make my exit without any further conversation.

"When can I see you again?" he asked.

"I'm not looking for a boyfriend," I told him, politely.

"I like you," he persisted.

"I'm very busy." I simply didn't have it in me to tell him straight out that I didn't like him.

He changed tack, explaining that he was a window cleaner and offering me a one off, free service. I refused politely, but firmly reiterating how busy I was.

"I'll come first thing, before you go out, 8 30 am, then you can go and I'll get on with it." Exasperated, I heard myself agreeing to

8 30 am the following day, when Scott would be at my house, cleaning my windows ... and he now had my address, as well.

The next day, instead of facing him, I got up early and went out. I went first to visit my mother, then to Jo's for a coffee, then I did my shopping, before returning home. Walking round the back way, something I did regularly as a way of bringing my early childhood living with my father to my present life, I opened the gate and to my utter astonishment, Scott was sitting on the ground with an intense look on his face. I could not believe he had sat there for over three hours, waiting for me. This was odd behaviour and I felt nervous and uncomfortable. The expression on his face scared me – it was more than determination – more like a cold, calculated resolve. But to do what?

I didn't know at that time – how could I have known – that he had confided in Mark only a couple of weeks earlier that he was looking for a girlfriend to latch onto for a place to live, because his wife was in the process of kicking him out.

Was that why he was so persistent – he wasn't even interested in me; he was just desperately looking for a place to live?

I knew he had crossed a boundary, invading my privacy in this way and I was shocked, but I didn't know how to handle the situation. I took a deep breath, apologised, then I let him into my home.

10

Chapter 10

Trying to hide the shock on my face, I now faced the fact that a difficult conversation was to be had. Confrontation and assertion were extremely difficult for me. Any reasonable person would have just gone home, getting the message that I wasn't interested. Not this man. He looked at me intensely. He certainly wasn't letting me off that easily.

I tried to act casually, as though nothing was wrong.

"Would you like a cup of tea for cleaning the windows?" I cringed inwardly at the sound of my own words, but they seemed to calm the anger in his face. Even though he hadn't actually done the windows, he accepted the tea and followed me inside.

Putting on the kettle in the kitchen, my mind was thinking fast. I gazed out of the window, to give myself a couple of minutes thinking time. *What an earth was I going to say to him?* I was going to have to tell him out right that I didn't like him, my stomach lurched at the thought.

When I finally walked into my living room, he was sitting on the chair closest to the window. His expression was clear in the sunlight; deep and intense. My discomfort increased.

He spoke first.

"I've had a bad life," he blurted, out of the blue.

I had a kind and gentle heart, much like my father's and was gullible at the best of the times, but this was not the time for me to be listening to his story of his past. I thought it strange that he was even choosing to tell me.

"Lots of people have," I told him. "You just have to move on." I was quoting Jo and Vanessa and my father, all the people in my life who'd tried to help me overcome my own difficulties. Not taking the cue from my disinterest, he carried on.

"My father is violent; he beat me and my mother, although I hate my mother, too." He described several situations, his words dripping with festered resentment and deep anger, all rooted, he claimed, in a lifetime of rejection from his parents.

"My mother abandoned me and allowed me to go into care … I wanted to go home. Everyone in my life has rejected me."

I was now faced with the even greater task of rejecting him, in view of everything he had just said.

"Can I see you again?" he asked.

"I'm busy," I told him, again.

His tone changed slightly, revealing a much more controlling and hostile version of himself.

"Doing what?" He was asking me to explain myself. I did.

"I am setting my own business up," I told him, feeling a mixture of pride and relief that I had actually had such a good a reason to use.

When I completed my beauty therapy course and successfully finished a placement, I had decided to set up a small mobile beauty therapy service in the small town where I lived. I already had a couple of customers and that would increase, if I had a little bit of financial investment. I had been invited to attend an interview the week after, to apply for a grant from the Princes' Trust. This would mean that I had access to financial support to pay the rent and bills in the setting up phase of the business, ensuring I could get by.

Without asking, he helped himself to one of my price lists, which was lying on the floor where I'd been working on my business plan the night before. I should have been continuing that work this morning, if only I hadn't put myself in the position of giving him my address.

"I'll have a massage." His eyes fixed on my face.

"I don't have any oil," I lied. He was not a genuine customer. I could see he was trying to push his way into my life. I was trying to keep my own boundaries. He offered to go and get some.

"I am *really* busy," I said, in the most forceful tone I felt I had the confidence to use at the time.

"Well, next time I come I will have one, then." I may have put him off this time, but he still wasn't giving up entirely.

I wanted this battle of wits to be over. It wasn't something I was strong at, or comfortable with; I just wanted him out of my house.

"OK," I replied. I was already confident in my own mind that there would be no massage and no next time. I just wanted him to leave.

He reluctantly stepped up and moved towards the door, taking his time. He paused for a moment at the door and I held my breath. Was he going to find another excuse to try to stay? He glanced at me, a dark, almost threatening glance, and left.

I kicked myself. I was not going to put myself in that position again.

It was a measure of how far I'd come in my life that, after about fifteen minutes, I had put the whole situation behind me.

I busied myself around my house, putting things away in my daughter's room before she came home from school. It was nearing the school summer holidays following her second year at school. As I picked up some clothes to put into the wash basket, I froze, someone was downstairs. Someone was in my house. I had left the back door unlocked and someone had walked in without knocking. *Who was it?* If it were the next-door neighbour, they would have shouted as they came in. I quietly moved to the top of the stairs, afraid.

"Who's there," I shouted, hoping the quiver in my voice wasn't noticeable.

"Michelle, it's me," Scott's voice called back. I walked down the stairs, dumbfounded. He had that same intense look on his face as he did when he left, only fifteen minutes earlier.

"Michelle," he said, his voice terse, "I can't get on with my work." I felt as though I was suffocating.

"I don't understand," he continued. I smiled weakly, trying to hide my confusion. What was he talking about?

"Are we girlfriend and boyfriend?" he demanded, "because you're acting as though we're not."

My mind spun. How could he get to this conclusion? I had already brushed him off twice. But before I had time to answer he, blurted out clumsily, "Can we be intimate?"

"No! no! no!" I was horrified. He hadn't even waited for an answer to the boyfriend/girlfriend question.

There was no way that I had led him on. Maybe I hadn't made it clear enough that I wasn't interested in him, even though I'd said I was busy now five or six times.

"Can I just kiss you then?"

Confusion, disbelief, fear, panic ... my thoughts and feelings engulfed me. I had no idea what was going on. Nothing like this had ever happened.to me before. In spite of my every instinct railing against it, I felt forced to allow him to kiss me, trying to turn my head so that his kiss landed on my cheek.

I felt so stupid. *Why didn't I use my voice to express myself?* Why did I feel so isolated, powerless and vulnerable that I defaulted to feeling like I *had* to pacify this man who gave me the creeps? My assertion and social skills were non existent. I had given Scott an inch and now he was going to take a thousand miles.

If I could have turned the clock back in my life and change things it would have been at this point, or, more probably, the day I met Jane again.

Whichever moment – Jane, or meeting Scott – two months later, I would be sitting in a prison cell, my father murdered.

I would later find out that Scott's claims about the abuse he suffered were true.

Before he was five-years-old, he witnessed his mother being beaten and would withdraw into himself. His father also hit him. His mother left, leaving him with his father and his girlfriend, who locked him in a room to starve. After he set a vehicle on fire, he was sent to a school psychiatrist. He was just six-years-old. He was placed in a school for children with behavioural difficulties. Following the psychological assessment, his father further rejected him, often telling him that he was mad. Following an allegation of abuse at the school, he was moved to an alternative school. No one visited him much, and he began to harbour a deep resentment for both of his parents. A loner by nature, at the age of fourteen he was returned to his father. He was never able to accept being sent away. His father continued to hit him in an attempt, the father claimed, to make him behave, or punish him for his bad behaviour. At the age of fifteen, he was old enough to be convicted for burglary and sent to a detention centre –

it didn't deter him from crime. For the next nineteen years, he racked up a string of convictions for burglary, fraud, deception, theft. He had met his wife in 1983, but by 1993, she was throwing him out. Then he met me.

I wondered whose father he was thinking of when he murdered my father: his or mine?

Chapter 11

Standing in the front of the mirror, in my old bedroom at my mother's house, I looked at my reflection and felt a sense of pride. I was trying on a smart blouse I had borrowed from Sarah and some dress trousers, to see what they looked like, in preparation for my interview the next day at the Prince's Trust Fund. I was determined to do well. I just needed a small helping hand to get me there. When I borrowed the blouse from Sarah the previous day, I'd told her about the weird encounter with Scott. She brushed it off, smiling positively.

"Don't worry about it, you worry too much ... maybe you should give him a chance," she said. She wasn't really listening to me, but her words made me doubt myself, momentarily; *Perhaps I was being too harsh on him?* My gut instinct told me otherwise and anyway, I didn't like him. For a start, he was eleven years older than me; I was twenty-two, he was thirty-three. I'd never gone out with anyone older than me and we had nothing in common.

I stayed at my mum's that night so she could take my daughter to school the next morning and I could catch an early train to Hull. My father's drug and alcohol use had worsened, it was no longer an option to ask him to look after my daughter. I was thinking about my father now and wished that I could be there with him, just like I had only a year ago. I felt helpless, watching him spiralling into a deep hole. I couldn't pull him out, or pull him to his senses. My thoughts, however, were brought sharply back to the bedroom by a loud hammering on my mother's front door. *Who the hell knocked like that?*

I could then hear my mum's regular, loud, over-exaggerated welcoming tone, followed by footsteps steps coming upstairs. *That was strange … why were they coming upstairs?* I heard Scott's voice and my stomach knotted.

"What are you doing here?" I demanded. My borrowed clothes had given me an air of confidence. I was not afraid to show my irritation at my mum for letting him in, yet again. She knew so well that I didn't like him and she was aware of the position I had been in, after him telling me his story of lifelong rejections.

It had been a week since I last saw him. My mother still revelled in situations that put me in an uncomfortable position, like this one. She left us together and went downstairs into the living room where my daughter was watching TV. He stared hard at me. Was I imagining it, or did he seem relieved that he knew where I was?

"What is it?" I demanded, again sharply. I was angry at yet another invasion and I wasn't as vulnerable here, as I was in my own home.

"What are you doing here?" he asked. I stared at him for a moment – he'd avoided answering my question by turning the focus back onto me. What's more, he spoke as if he had a *right* to know what I was doing and why.

"I'm going for an interview, why?" I should have told him it was none of his business, but once again, he'd caught me off guard. I was beginning to feel trapped. In spite of everything, he seemed panicky, as though he had walked out of some kind of crisis. He needed something, that was clear, but what did he want from me? It had been a week now since that strange visit to my house; we were not in a relationship; this was only the third time I had seen him. Anyone else would have just told him to go to hell, but not me.

I just wanted him out of the house, so that I could prepare for my interview.

I remained just inside my bedroom, holding the door open with my arm as a barrier, making it clear he wasn't staying.

"I am busy," I told him, in an attempt to reinforce my body language. An angry expression flashed across his face.

"When can I see you?" he demanded abruptly.

"I don't know," I replied. Surely I was making it clear? After a couple of minutes, he left reluctantly. *Why can't he just get the message?* I thought to myself.

"Why did you let him in?" I asked Mum, annoyed.

"He's a nice man," she replied.

"Well you might think he's nice, but I don't like him, so please don't let him in again."

I knew it was useless. If I told my Mum I didn't like something, she would do it anyway and vice versa.

"Don't be awful," she said, trying to make me feel ashamed for not liking him, or that by not liking him, I was doing something wrong.

She could trigger my self doubt and anxiety like no one else. The relentless self judgement kicked in instantly. *What if she was right and I was a bad person for not liking Scott?* I questioned my own rights to ask someone to leave me alone and wondered if my decision not to have anything to do with him was correct. Why couldn't she ever support any decision I made?

What I really needed to hear was: Michelle, if you don't like him, you need to make it very clear. Tell him you're not letting him in your house and if he doesn't like it, then just call the police; don't give him an inch, because people like that will take a mile.

~~Instead, I saw my defeated~~ reflection in the mirror, rendered helpless by my own behaviour. Lying in bed that night, self doubt crowded my mind and the hope for tomorrow's interview evaporated.

The next day, however, the train journey seemed to dissolve away the feelings of the night before and my resilience to fight back once again emerged. I didn't realise, at that time, but it was the key to my survival – past, present and future. I located the office near the station quite quickly and I sat in the small waiting room, mentally preparing myself. I looked up to see a large, happy looking man studying me. I was nervous, desperate to do well. He smiled reassuringly.

"Yes, you're accepted! The course starts next week," he boomed, just twenty minutes later. He was so kind and empathic, it seemed he'd told me as soon as possible, to relieve my anxiety.

I felt elated, so proud that I had achieved something, finally, which gave me such a sense of pride. I'd completed my college course with several distinctions; I had plans in place to set up my mobile beauty therapy service; I'd gained financial support from the Princes Trust Fund, including a two week course to equip me with sound support and business planning to ensure my best chance at success. I couldn't wait to get home to tell my mother, Sarah and most importantly, my father.

As soon as I got home, I went to visit my father to tell him the news, knowing how genuinely proud he would be of me. I also wanted to see how he was. Perhaps my hope would rub off and I could convince him that there is always something positive around the corner. Walking up to the door of what I still thought of as my home, I held the handle but didn't turn it. I heard his so-called friend Lewis's voice inside and I halted in my tracks. I hated him. I'd heard stories of him robbing vulnerable people and suspected he'd emptied my dad's pockets on at least one occasion, when my dad was too drugged to realise what was happening. I went back to my car. Opening the car door, I put my excited news on hold and decided to wait outside for Lewisto leave. Watching the house, I saw a woman hesitate when she went to the gate. A local company operated a weekly pay scheme for household items such as quilts, etc. I guessed she was one of their payment collectors. I wound the window down.

"Excuse me," I called.

"Yes," she smiled, relieved to see a friendly face.

"Are you going to that house for money?"

"Yes," she said.

"How much does he owe you in total?"

"Twenty-five pounds," she answered, looking confused. I opened my purse and gave her the money.

I had heard recently that Lewis had started injecting my father with amphetamines. It was something he had not done before and he was now turning up daily. The drugs he had once offered my father for free, in apparent friendship, he now used against him, taking his benefits. I blamed him for my Dad's addiction getting worse and desperately I wanted to help him get out of the hole Lewis had created. I had no proof, of course, my father, by then, was too damaged by the drugs and alcohol. All I had to go on were his confused accounts, reports from his older friends and my own observation of my father's rapid decline after this man came into his life.

When I finally did walk into the house, my father looked up at me confused, wondering who was now walking in.

"You OK, Dad?" I asked. He began to cry.

"We can do this, Dad," I tried to reassure him.

"Let's try and get you a flat. Somewhere smaller that you can manage." I put on the kettle to make him a cup of tea. I genuinely believed that a move would be the answer to all his problems. My daughter had even drawn a picture of a new house for him, with a happy face smiling out of the window and we put it on his wall above the kitchen door. I looked at that picture now and back at his lost face, as I tried to pull him out of his sinking depression. My good news seemed to lift him up.

"When you're rich, I'll have a Grandad house attached to yours," he laughed and I saw a glimpse of my old father returning.

It was in that moment the door opened. I thought it was Lewis again, and didn't know whether to be relieved or furious when Scott walked in. A look of agitation crossed his face when he saw us having a heart to heart. I picked up my father's clothes to take home with me to wash, trying to distract myself from my shock that he was here and knew how to locate me. It was obvious he was here for me; he told me had been looking for me and my mum had directed him here. He also seemed familiar with my father and the code for friends to just walk into the house, a code that had been violated by Lewis and now Scott.

"Michelle," he said, "I have been looking all over for you, what time did you get back?" My father, on the other hand, was pleased to see him. In fact, he was pleased to see anyone and he wanted nothing more than for me to meet a nice man to look after me, after I'd been hurt in my past relationship.

"Sit down, sit down," my father smiled at him, encouraging him to stay. "Michelle, get him a cup of tea." I went into the kitchen and returned with the drink, then left them together, taking my father's washing with me. My father didn't walk me to the door, kissing me on the cheek like he normally did. He was too engaged with Scott; it was the first time he had met him.

Scott went on to form an allegiance with both my father and brother, often taking them weed to smoke and staying for hours. It was as though he was forming alliances with all those close around me. I now had not only him to fend off, but my families' views and ideas about him, too. They all liked him and the only one who didn't was me.

Chapter 12

My mother and I had been invited to my uncle's place in Plymouth as guests at my cousin's wedding. It was exciting for me to be included and take my daughter, on one of our first holidays, to their home for the wedding. Just a couple of days before the wedding, when I was discussing the plans with my mother, Scott turned up, unannounced, again.

"I've come for a cup of tea," he announced, walking in the back door. "I am on a break from work, so I thought I would pop in." *Wasn't he always on a break?* I thought. My mother welcomed him in. I put on the kettle, what else could I do? Then I heard my mother inviting him to come with us on holiday for the wedding. Agitation and disappointment surged through me. Our first holiday was being spoiled before it had even begun.

"Come with us, Scott, it would be lovely to have you!" I saw that glint of laughter in eyes, taunting me in front of him.

"No!" I was not having any of it.

"If I want to invite anyone to the wedding as my guest, I will do the inviting." I surprised myself with the strength of my words.

That strange visit to my house played through my mind. That reluctant kiss… how I regretted it, blaming myself for giving him that tiny opening. I had quickly tried to pull it back, but he had already created a reality in his mind that he seemed determined to pursue. He had shown me a tattoo on his chest of a huge grim reaper and spoken of attacking his wife's abuser in the past. He seemed to think my rejection of him must have been because I, too, had been abused in the past. I told him that although I was taken advantage of when I was only fifteen there was nothing in my past that could be described as abuse of that nature.

"Tell me who it was," he'd said. "I'll kill him." I certainly didn't tell him who it was, wondering how the conversation had even got to this point.

My mother's voice brought me back to the present.

"Don't be awful, Michelle, it would be lovely to have Scott come to the wedding with us." Scott was clearly enjoying the alliance with my mother and quickly sensed her lack of loyalty as a mother, to me. I didn't budge.

"No," I reasserted myself in a less hostile way, knowing and seeing Scott's dark eyes holding back his obvious negative thoughts. I looked at his face and gave him an explanation, trying to appease him.

"I'm sorry, but I'm going alone. I don't know you well enough to take you to my cousin's." I had only known him now for a few weeks and he was already intrusive and frightening.

"Who is going to look after the animals?" my mother continued, as if nothing had happened. I had a bird, a rabbit and some fish which all needed tending to.

"I can do it," Scott offered.

"I'm going to ask Julie, my neighbour."

"But I'm in this area every day cleaning windows," he said. "You might as well just give me the key and I will pop in on my rounds – it'll only take me two minutes." I looked at him, not knowing how to answer.

"Oh, let him do it, for God's sake," my mother snapped, as if I was being childish. I stalled there and then.

Hesitantly, I reached up to the top shelf where I kept the spare key and handed it to him. He smiled gleefully, and left just a couple of minutes after I handed him the key. Packing for our trip later that evening, I was glad I hadn't given in to allow Scott to come with us. For now, I was happy and excited.

The holiday was all I wished for and more. It was then my mum's first signs of poor physical heath started to show and she spent most of the holiday resting, leaving me free to enjoy myself with my daughter. My uncle and his wife had been great hosts; we had been taken to so many amazing places throughout our stay, but before I knew it, we were on the train back to Bridlington. Seeing another town left me thinking about the deprived town in which I lived and for the first time in my life, I saw it with an outsider's eyes. I wanted to succeed and move away.

Scott was still at my house when I got home. I wasn't at all pleased to see him and I let it show. But when I walked into my kitchen I saw that a lovely plant had been placed there. How thoughtful, I thought, especially when I have been so off with him. For a second I began to consider that he might just be a nice person, after all and was trying to be nice friend to me – it was me who was always ungrateful to him. I felt bad. Then I saw a new picture on the wall.

"Is that yours?" I asked, before walking in any further from the kitchen. He looked at me without answering. I opened the living room door; there was a row of cannabis plants, on my living room window, for all the world to see.

"What are they doing here?" I turned to look at him. He stared back impassively, and it dawned on me he had not answered either of my questions.

"They're only plants," he said, looking at me like I was being irrational.

"Yes, I know, but they're cannabis plants and they're illegal, they are in my house, on my window sill and they do not belong to me."

I could hear frustration, bordering on hysteria, in my own voice.

Scott frowned, as if I should be ashamed of myself for speaking to him that way.

I was already starting to feel tired and suffocated. I took a deep breath and plucked up the courage to look at him straight in the face.

"Right, what are your things doing here?" I demanded.

"I'm living here," he said, calmly, not even remotely concerned that this was my house.

"What do you mean, you're living here?" This had gone way too far.

"Someone needed my flat," he answered, dismissively.

"I'm sorry, Scott, but I'm not stupid; people don't give up flats because someone else needs it. I want you out of here as soon as possible and in the meantime, I want my key back."

"I'm going to need it," he replied in a flat, unconcerned voice and that was that. He went to put the TV on and I took my daughter to bed with me. She had now lost her bedroom to Scott while we were away. He never returned the key. He knew I was vulnerable and powerless – he had sucked in all of my family onto his side – I'd have no support to get him out.

He did agree that he would look for somewhere else to live, but didn't know exactly when that would be. I hated his odd presence and wanted him out of my house as soon as possible. I had to try to continue with my life with him in my house, totally invading my life. Had my father been in the same mind-set that he was only a year ago, he would have come and changed the locks for me, but his mind was not his own and I was alone in this situation.

Scott spent most of his time with my brother and the rest of his time with Jane. I was glad I didn't see him that often and when I did, there was no more hiding my intolerance of him.

A couple of days later, however, finishing my course with the Princes Trust, I was sitting in the classroom feeling uplifted again. I was conversing and making some great links for my new business. One person asked if they could use me on a contract basis for makeup applications for their new photography enterprise. I felt I had overcome a major hurdle by securing a first, good customer and leaving the building, I was happy. I became disorientated at the exit and suddenly realised I was unsure of the direction of the train station. It wasn't an area of Hull I was familiar with, as I had never ventured far out of its centre before.

"Can you just point me in the direction of the station," I asked another student on his way out from another class.

Just when he was in the middle of explaining to me, I looked to the end of the path and there was Scott looking angry and stern. I couldn't believe my eyes. *It couldn't be, surely!* It was. How did he know I was here and how did he have the exact address and my leaving time? Before I had chance to think, I realised his anger was directed at the young man giving me directions. I felt overpowered and consumed. He was obviously going through my private letters.

"Thanks," I said to the man, bringing his directions to an abrupt end. "I think I have a lift after all." He looked up at Scott and nodded.

"No problem," he smiled and walked away. I wished I could have walked away too, to have a normal life away from Scott, but instead, I walked over to where he was standing.

How an earth was I going to get this man out of my life? What the hell was he doing here, forty miles away from his so called window cleaning round? What made him think it was OK to meet me here?

I had absolutely no one to go to for help.

Everybody had taken Scott's side. I was the bad, the ungrateful *girlfriend*. My mother, father, brother, Lewis and even Jane had commented on my discontented behaviour towards him. He had been so helpful, according to them, giving my brother a job window cleaning. He had been partly responsible they believed, for calming down my brother's drug use, which was more chaotic than my father's. Even my own father, who had never in his life spoken ill of me, seemed displeased with me, or at least, that's what I was being told.

From what I had heard, Scott was twisting the truth that he had moved in without my consent and his obvious growing obsession, to the story that he was trying to make an honourable woman of me, trying to take me away from the fact that I was a single parent. Scott was a Jehovah's Witness and although he gave his judgmental remarks out, he certainly didn't abide by his own standards. I told him of my own religion, in response to being judged by him.

"Being kind and honest with people and caring for their needs makes me a good person, it's not a label I could use to say I was like a Jehovah's Witness or a Christian, for example." And to me, at that time, although I had made more than my share of not so great decisions, that's exactly who I was.

Jane visited me one day in my home, when I hadn't visited her for a while.

"Why are you treating Scott awful?" she demanded, almost sneering. "You need to be careful." There was no mistaking it, her words were a threat, one that rang alarm bells in my mind.

"I don't like him," I told her. She stood up, leaning on my wall in an intimidating way. I pretended not to notice. "If you like him, you go out with him."

"I don't want him," she scowled at me. "I am just warning you, he is saying some awful things about you and if I was you, I'd treat him properly. He is round at my house every day talking about you and some of the things aren't nice."

I suspected Scott could be violent, although I hadn't actually seen him being violent. There was something constantly simmering just below the surface and it terrified me to think what might happen if it ever erupted.

Sitting in his car going back to Bridlington, the happiness the day had given me drained away and I became a shell again. The words I wanted to say to Scott did not come out. He seemed to be believing the pretence he had built for others about our relationship and my bad behaviour. He drove, stone faced, emanating judgement and anger. He clearly believed he was a victim of something I had done.

Sometimes, it was as if, when he had an idea in his head, he would zone out and not hear anyone else's input or opinions. Or was it just mine and he didn't care for them? He had become strongly positioned in my broken family and I wanted to shout out to someone to help me.

Once, in desperation, not knowing who else to turn to, I went to his friend, Mark, for advice and for help. After listening to my concerns about the strange and invading behaviour, he agreed to help me. He knew Scott a little better than I did, but not much.

"He just turned up here one day," he told me. "I don't know much about him either."

"Can you put him up here? He says he is looking for somewhere to live, but I don't believe him." Mark was reluctant at first, but he agreed, after I practically begged him.

"I don't want him here, Michelle," Mark confessed, "he's not really my friend, but I'll do it on a short term to help you." I couldn't wait to tell Scott that I had found him somewhere to live.

"I'm not going anywhere," he said with a straight face and carried on regardless, in my house.

I called Mark later that day from my mum's. "He said he's not leaving," I said in desperation, hoping Mark would help me to convince him to leave.

"He's here now Michelle, I'll ask him." I listened to the conversation over the phone. Scott agreed to move out of my house!

I was afraid to get my hopes up, it had sounded far too easy and I guessed he was just saying it, without having any intention to follow through. I was right.

When he returned to my house that evening, he showed no sign of moving out, but his hostility and anger towards me intensified. I couldn't ask Mark to do any more, without thinking I was becoming a nuisance. I didn't know him that well. I was beginning to lose hope.

Chapter 13

Scott had refused to leave that night, without even a glance or explanation. I found it difficult to get to sleep, feeling uneasy and unsafe in my own home. The police would not help, they would just tell me to change the locks and I had no money to do that. The only person who could have helped was my father and I was losing him now, not only to Lewis, but because of Scott, too. I had just got off to a light sleep when I heard someone banging on my door in the middle of the night. The first thought that came into my head was my father. There was something wrong with him. *No, no, no,* I thought. I wasn't ready to lose him. I ran down the stairs and opened the door quickly, to see my mother standing there, frantic, with obvious bad news.

"It's Neil, he's ill," she cried in desperation.

After asking a neighbour to look after my daughter, I picked up my father, who was just as upset and helpless as my mother. Despite years of Neil being abusive and aggressive towards me, we knew we were all going to be there for him, without any hesitation. My Mum told me that Neil was in Cottingham Hospital. However, on our way there, he had been transferred to the Royal Infirmary in Hull. Just as a nurse at Cottingham was explaining that Neil's condition had deteriorated rapidly, leaving them no choice but to transfer him, another nurse approached us. She spoke directly to me.

"We have had your boyfriend on the phone, he is being very aggressive and wants to know what is going on, but I couldn't tell him." Her tone made it clear Scott's behaviour was unacceptable.

Over recent weeks, Scott was not only obsessive about me, he had also become obsessive about Neil. In fact, they had started to do everything together.

We couldn't even have a family crisis without him impinging into my life.

"He is not my boyfriend," I said to the nurse.

"Michelle, don't be awful," my mother said.

I didn't answer her. Now was not the time.

When we got to the infirmary we had to wait for the doctor to explain to us what was wrong; we began to fear for Neil's life. In that life changing moment, I felt the first stirring of empathy for my brother in a long time. *Had I been a bad sister? Had I tried hard enough?* I promised myself that, if he got well, I would be a better sister. To make matters worse, I had to leave the intensive care unit to find somewhere to buy alcohol for my father. He had become so dependent on it that, without it, he would start to become ill. That night, I saw him as selfish first and his addiction last instead of the other way around. Of course, he was selfish, that is what addictions do. The drug controls and takes over the person, ensuring that need is fed before anything else. However, when I gave him the bottle, my tone was the worst it had ever been with him.

"Here," I told him harshly, thrusting the bottle towards him, before I walked back into the hospital room. My father became consumed with his bottle. My mother on the other hand was using the situation to socialise with other people, talking to everyone in the room, like she was waiting for a bus. She hardly looked at Neil at all. I was there, left acting like the only responsible adult. When I came out for a rest, my father was laid flat out on the sofa in the waiting room, intoxicated. I always carried on, regardless of what other people thought. It didn't bother me. I had never been ashamed of my father. But on this night, he was at the height of losing his dignity.

After we had come home and returned the next day, Scott was not long behind us. It was all I needed right now. He was unwelcome and I made it obvious, but he was there for Neil and it was apparent that he had made it his right to be there.

The doctor informed me of Neil's progress, without asking who the next of kin was.

"He's lucky," he said, as Neil started to pull around. "He had a blood clot on his brain, we have removed it and we can only hope for a successful recovery, but he must be strong. Any more drugs and he might not be so lucky next time."

In the time before he started to recover, I had blamed everyone, including my father, in that brief moment. I also blamed my mother, thinking she hadn't done enough for Neil. I blamed myself too. We were told he was dying. I blamed us all.

In the days after Neil began to recover, my mother and I discussed supporting Neil and my Dad to get clean. They had always triggered each other off in the past, when they tried to get clean before. One would weaken, whilst one would be strong, but then both would give in and start using again. It was something that had happened three or four times that year so far. I asked Neil if he wanted to stay with me whilst he got better. It was the first time, in my life, I had put him before my father. It didn't mean I loved him more than my father, it just meant that he was the priority at that moment. It seemed more critical at that stage to keep him clean. He had been in hospital for a few days, so the worst was obviously over, he just needed some more time in the community without drugs.

He had only been with me for a couple of hours before he nipped out, returning just over an hour later, paralytic from drinking. I had to get him out of my house, he was swearing at me and pushing me and I was afraid for my own safety. He was repeating the things that Scott said about me.

"Everybody hates you, now," he gloated. He talked about how glad he was that Scott had come along to expose me. Before the day was over, he was back with my father. I was helpless to help him and I didn't see him much after that. Our relationship returned pretty much to what it was.

Scott, on the other hand, continued to see and visit him every day as their strange friendship took off. The shock of seeing Neil so aggressive with me made me make peace with my father's growing addictions. Making peace meant accepting that it wasn't my choice whether he gave up his addictions or not. The only person who could help him was himself. I often begged and begged my father to come off drugs. A couple of days later, he came over to see me and whilst I walked with him and my daughter to a nearby park, I opened up to him.

"Dad, I am not going to ask you to come off drugs any more. When the time is right time is for you, you'll do it," I told him. It was a strange moment; he looked sort of disappointed, but I had learned some very hard lesson at this young age. It was his choice to make and not mine. I had now to get on with my life.

In the following days, Scott's invasion of my life escalated, because he had now recruited my brother. At times, I would see them following me about in their car, they had even taken the roof rack off, so I didn't notice it. Neil would often shout out of the window, hurling abuse at me if I saw them and asked them what they were doing. I tried to get my life back on track and agreed to go out with my friend Sarah and an ex-boyfriend Shaun, who asked if he could come along. I was fond of Shaun; he was a nice guy. It wasn't a date, it was a group night out and myself, Sarah and Shaun were all at Sarah's mum's house, waiting for Sarah to finish getting ready. Scott and Neil turned up a short while later. I didn't know they were there at the at first, but when I went out to my car with Shaun to get a bag, Scott jumped out of his car, telling me to get in his car, brandishing a huge spanner as a weapon. My brother got out, drunk – he was also holding a weapon.

I couldn't believe what was happening. Sarah's mum came out from the house, in response to the commotion.

"Get inside Michelle," she commanded.

I didn't leave her on her own, but watched her shouting at the two grown men.

"Who do you think you are, the pair of you, intimidating young, vulnerable women?" I started to walk to the front door to get Sarah's dad, knowing how much danger his wife was in, when I heard the car revving up. I blamed myself. I had brought the danger here. I walked back just in time to witness the car being driven towards Shaun and a child who had run out of the house during the incident. Shaun not only managed to pick up the child before the car got to him, but also managed to hurdle over a fence, saving both himself and the child. The car reversed and screeched off.

Back inside the house, all I could say was sorry. I internalised the events, as I had always done. The police were called out to what was being treated as a serious crime. It was finally over, I thought. The police will pick up and arrest Scott and I will finally be free of him.

I went to stay at my mother's for a few days. Scott had two cars – he had left one car parked outside my mother's, as if his presence was still there.

"Go home," my mother told me, out of nowhere. "I don't want you to stay."

The police did nothing. Scott was not even questioned, let alone arrested. They didn't even pay him a visit, despite us telling the police where he would be and despite making it clear he had nearly killed two people. Only one day after the attack, I had to go home. Scott made an unforgettable further attempt to explain why he was staying at my house – he told me about his wife, never having even mentioned her in all the time he was forcing himself into my life.

"You didn't ask," he responded, nonchalantly, to my shocked questions. Then he told me about his twelve-year-old daughter, still at home with his wife. He claimed that the twelve-year-old was flirting and coming onto him. Horrified, I challenged him, telling him I didn't think his daughter would be flirting with him, but he was adamant. She was definitely flirting – she wore a see through night dress and would sit on his knee. It was similar to what he'd said about me, when he'd claimed I had been flirting with him at Marks' house, when, in reality, I had spoken to him like I would any other human being. This logic was now making me feel sick.

"I want you to leave." It was the firmest I had been with him, with my mothering instinct in full attack, I turned on him. He looked shocked, as if he could not understand what was wrong with what he had said. He making these claims as if they were real and normal facts. He was clearly sick. Knowing I was fighting a losing battle, I packed a few of my daughter's things and mine and headed back to my mum's. I had to keep my daughter safe and now, I did not feel safe at all.

I must have looked desperate, because she allowed me to stay. I couldn't tell my mum; she had suffered nervous breakdowns, so I kept it all in, living, now, in real fear. The police had done nothing after his previous attack. I felt alone – there was no one I could turn to for help.

Tolerating Scott because I was too weak to stand up to him was over. There would be no more pussy footing about. I wanted him out.

What I didn't know in this time was that he was spending a lot of time with Jane, discussing the situation with her.

What I also didn't know, and wouldn't find out until much later, was that Jane, he claimed, had told him my father abused me. Jane was a mixed up, chaotic woman who loved to intimidate and cause drama, but I had no idea she would make something like that up. One other thing I didn't know was that he was apparently planning to kill me. I'd heard that he told Lewis he was going to petrol bomb my house.

I stayed with my mother for a week, trying to come up with a plan to get rid of him that couldn't fail. During that week, I heard that he was seeking revenge for what he believed (and tried to convince anyone who would listen) had been my terrible treatment of him. He was also obsessed with keeping my brother safe and was with him at all times. I popped into my father' a few times during the week I stayed with my mother.

"I've had enough of you," my mother announced, at the end of the week. "You're going home."

"Mum, please, don't make me go home."

"Go and get your house back, it's your house. Now get out."

That night I went to Jo, my closest friend from college. In a desperate attempt to stay away from my own house, I begged her.

"Please let me stay, Jo." She came to the door.

"I can't, flower," she said, kindly "my boyfriend is here." Jo's boyfriend was staying the night in her small flat.

"I'll sleep anywhere."

"Sorry, flower." I left, helplessly. I understood. She had no space.

I had nowhere to go but home, with my daughter. And no one to help me to get him out, not even the police.

14

Chapter 14

I witnessed my father's horrific murder on Thursday September 9th, 1993, a day I can't and won't ever forget. It is the day that is forever imprinted upon my mind with an unspeakable horror. A day that my reality became a living nightmare. I am unable to wake from Thursday September 9th, the very same day I was going to and should have taken back not only my house, but also my life, that had been totally invaded by this man. A man who cared nothing for me, but, I felt, fed into and from my isolation and vulnerability.

I was to do that alone, without any assistance from anyone.

The day after I had pleaded with Jo to let me stay began with me literally bumping into Scott in my kitchen. I have played that day over and over again in my mind, willing me to make different moves at various points of that day, to prevent that horror from occurring. I would have given anything to be able to go back and change it, to find some way of getting help. But, every time I replay those events, I still sense that isolation and helplessness and still find it difficult to locate that help, if I was still faced with the same, specific set of circumstances. After twenty years, I still feel that same intensity of horror and I have no doubt, at all, that it will continue for the rest of my life.

One of my biggest regrets was not fighting back. I had the chance, at one point, but torn between needing to protect others that I also loved at home and terror for my own life, I hesitated. Looking back now, that is one of the biggest regrets I have. To have taken the risk and tried to fight back would have been, without a doubt, the better option than what I was to go on to experience. I should have protected my father, just like he protected me when I was younger, from my mother. I had protected him in many situations but here – in this critical moment – I failed to act and so I write the hardest part of the story; explaining why I did nothing at all to protect my father – frozen and helpless, never wanting the attack to happen, a powerless, horrified observer.

Standing at the sink, I switched off the tap and placed the glass on the draining board to dry. I didn't even hear Scott come into the kitchen. In fact, it wasn't until I spun around quickly to head for the door, that I literally bumped into his six-foot tall presence. I gasped; I was already on edge and was trying to leave the house as quickly as I could, before he had a chance to see me. I failed. I tried to compose myself, but was suddenly exposed. I couldn't guess his next move. I had never been able to. He didn't move or apologise for blocking my path; instead he looked at me intensely. *Why wouldn't he just leave me alone?* I had come to feel that he only pretended that he liked me, really, it was all about control. His obsession for me had turned into an obsession for revenge for my rejection of him. Instead of apologising for his obviously unwelcome presence, he spoke to me about the other person he had recently become obsessed with, my brother. Even my mother had started to complain about that obsession to me. She and my father had been left uncomfortable in her home when Scott had sneaked up on them both – he had clearly been watching my father's movements.

"Your brother has been using drugs again," he said, a strange tone in his voice. I felt like he was trying to draw me into a reaction.

"That's up to him," I replied, without making eye contact, still waiting for him to move out of my way, so that I could leave the house.

"Well," he continued, his eyes never leaving my face, "Lewis and your Dad pinned him down and injected him with a cocktail of drugs. You know what the doctors have said."

I didn't believe a word of it. He was using his couple of weeks' experience of my father and brother to try to plant doubts in my mind. I knew that my father couldn't even inject himself. Lewis always helped him with that and in all my life, I had never known my father to be violent. In fact, it was the other way around. My brother was the violent character. Why Neil would have to be held down to take drugs made no sense, either. I wondered what Scott's motives were for trying to upset or make me angry in this particular way. Uneasiness crept over me, it had become my role to be the responsible parent in the family; my sense of duty must have shown as a reluctant emotion sweeping across my face. Scott picked up on it and offered his assistance:

"I'll give you a lift to your father's" he said, picking up his car keys.

"It's OK, I can walk." I didn't trust him one iota. It really was nothing to do with him and I knew he was interfering for his own reasons, whatever they might be.

"I'm going there anyway," he persisted. I accepted that lift. I'm not sure why. Perhaps in my isolation I tried to make my enemy a friend, to ensure my safety. Perhaps because it was easier than disagreeing with him, giving him a reason to cause me more problems. He was already overpowering me.

Coming out of the school after I had dropped my daughter off, I saw him and Jane talking by the roadside; she had dropped off her daughter at the same school.

"Come over for a coffee," she invited. I was as keen on seeing her, as I was Scott. I made a vague response about stopping by later. I told Scott to drop me off at my father's first. He was reluctant.

"You've told her you're going," he said, dropping me off right outside Jane's door. I felt at that point that I had little choice, my intention was to have a quick coffee before I went to see my father, to keep the peace with her. She was as domineering as Scott, albeit in a different way. Before he left, he came in to tell Jane that I didn't even want to see her. I found myself having to explain to her.

"I just wanted to see if everything was OK at my father's."

"Do you think you're too good for me or even Scott?" she sneered. It had been an accusation she made constantly since I'd first met her

"No, not at all, I just wanted to see my Dad. Anyway, I'm here now and I'll stay for a coffee."

Scott went to get on with his work and, momentarily, I was relieved.

"I can't get on with my work," he announced, minutes later. "I'm wondering if Neil is OK." I didn't know at that time, but Scott had lost a brother following his release from a prison sentence. The rest of the family hadn't really bonded with him and I have no way of knowing whether he had bonded with the brother he had lost. *Was he replacing that brother with mine?* When I did go over to my father's, Scott wasn't far behind, following me.

"What's happened, Dad?" I asked my father, when I finally arrived at his house. Lewis stood beside him, watching my every expression, knowing my disapproval of him. I looked at him and smiled to appease him, but I hated him. My father went along with the role reversal of me being the parent in the living room. If it hadn't been for Scott's presence behind me, I would have probably just put the kettle on as I normally did, making my dad a cup of tea with his three sugars. Although the last couple of weeks had been difficult, my relationship with my father was still as strong as ever. Scott was trying to cause an argument, I realised that now; he kept butting into the conversation from behind me, maliciously adding extra details, but my voice remained soft and calm. I questioned my father about the drugs and asked him if he was thinking about the consequences of drugs on Neil's health. I followed that conversation up by asking about his motivation.

"I thought you were going to get a flat?" was all I could think of to say. Looking up on his wall at the picture my daughter had drawn for him, I realised I was still a child at heart. My father was quiet. He wasn't antagonistic. Scott continued his attempt to make the situation into an argument, but my heart wasn't in it. I wanted to help my Dad, I really did, but I was learning fast about addictions in the last couple of weeks; most importantly, that I had to let him make his own decisions. I looked at Lewis again. I wanted to shout at him. All I really wanted to say was, 'What have you given my father? This man who had dignity, the man who brought me up with morals, what have you done to him?' Lewis cared nothing for my father's life or his dignity.

"Oh, don't lecture me," my father sighed. I had become a nag. Here I was again, performing what I believed to be my duty, being drawn into this situation for a reason I didn't really understand.

"He *has* been giving Neil drugs, look he's under the influence now." Scott pushed me in the direction of the kitchen.

I walked into the kitchen and momentarily, my heart went out to my brother. I knew he needed no encouragement to take drugs. *How could I make him see sense?* He was so clearly under the influence of something and was in the middle of painting the kitchen. The whole scene was bizarre.

"What are you doing? I don't know why you are bothering," I told him. He turned around and swore at me. He was just as violent as ever. I ran back into the living room, seeking safety in my father. Neil's abuse and name calling catapulted into full force within minutes and I was left fearing for my safety. I was crying like a little girl, but now I was beginning to feel frustrated at my helplessness.

That was why I started arguing with my father, it was the only reason I had ever argued with my father, which up to that point had been only a few times in my whole life. The truth was there was no reason, most of the time, to argue with him.

"Tell him Dad," I sobbed, as my twenty-seven-year-old brother, probably the strongest man in the room, moved threateningly towards me. I was afraid. Scott seemed to exacerbate my brother's violence where I was concerned. I was suddenly the little girl again and my father was the parent, but I am sure, to this day, he felt as helpless as I did. He was a frail man in comparison to Neil, his son, over whom he had no control.

"You know what Neil's like," he said, irritation hiding his fear, "stay out of his way."

In the heat of the fear and frustration, I felt cheated by my own father, he should have protected me. Neil had become not only violent to me, but also more violent to my father, who had suffered so much more from Neil than I had. I hadn't seen much of it, but when I did, I felt powerless to protect my father. Our argument was small in comparison to those my father had had with Neil, himself.

Yet my father had been just as childish as I was being now, only a few weeks previously, when my mum asked me to get her purse back. She told me he had stolen from her when his addiction was worsening. Because I had located it in his house and returned it to my mum, he had returned all the presents that I had ever bought him and left them outside my mother's house on the same day. I was heartbroken. I didn't understand that his emotions were so much more difficult for him to deal with, more because of the drugs than alcohol. I had returned the gifts when he calmed down but today, in my hurt and disappointment, I gathered them all up, including his beloved guitar and took them away with me. I had never before behaved so childishly, but today was the peak of everything. Neil was threatening me, Scott was taking over my life, my father had failed to protect me and the only person not involved, but whom I could already feel gloating at my distress, was my mum.

Returning to Jane's, I told her that things had not gone well. I was disappointed with myself. She made me a coffee. Scott came in and told me to try again with Neil, who was now on his own and angry with me. With his persuasion of the need to put things right with my brother, through loyalty as his friend, I went back over to try and appease and smooth things over with Neil. By now, however, he was in a rage. He knew I had taken the guitar I had bought and he tried to attack me as soon as I arrived. I felt as much in danger now as I did the day he'd attacked me in my own home, when he'd come out of hospital. He lunged at me repeatedly. I had to run and hide behind the furniture before his big fists reached me. As soon as I had the chance, I bolted out into the back garden. Overloaded now with emotions of fear and anger towards my brother I looked for a brick – it was stupid, but I just wanted to throw something at the house in sheer fear and frustration. It was then I saw the syringes that he had thrown out into the garden.

For the first time in my life, I was driven to considering committing a violent act at the height of being physically threatened by my brother. I scanned the garden quickly for a brick, but I couldn't find one. It was irrational and ridiculous – a part of me knew that, but another part was past caring. Neil had got away with verbally and emotionally abusing me all my life and today, I had had enough of him. In that moment of irrational, emotional overload, I'd had enough of them all, but especially Neil. I hated him. Unable to find anything to throw to vent my fears and frustration, I made for Jane's again, but as I started out, I saw the local bobby and ran up to him in an emotional mess.

"My brother," I gulped. "He's a drugs user and he's thrown all his syringes into the back garden." I was telling tales on my brother, like a child. I had never gone to the police about anyone before, with the exception of the incident with my daughter and the one with Scott just over a week before. The policeman didn't seem particularly interested and I ran on towards Jane's.

"What's up?" she asked when I arrived, shaking, at her door. I told her what had happened.

"I was that angry," I told her, "If there had been a brick in the garden, I would have broken the window." I was confused by her reaction.

"Wait a minute," she smiled, calmly. She disappeared into her back garden and returned with a brick in her hand. She would later deny handing me the brick.

"I don't feel like doing it now." The initial anger had dissipated. If I could have described my feelings then, I would have said I felt lost and confused.

"Do it," she said commanded, authoritatively, "It will make you feel better." I was stunned. Although I knew she wasn't my friend, deep down, I still thought it was wrong that she would try to escalate the situation. But, I still wasn't thinking clearly. Jane was staring at me – she expected to be obeyed. Even though I knew it was wrong, I took the brick and threw it in the window, then ran back to Jane to show her that I was complying with her. I couldn't take any more aggression. She looked satisfied.

Scott came back to Jane's ten minutes later.

"Did you throw a brick through the window?" he asked, furiously. "It nearly hit me! The police came and Neil wants to kill you. We all had to calm him down, including the officer." The day was a complete mess. I hung my head in my hands.

"I've had enough." I said quietly.

And I really meant it. By that, I meant that I wanted to pack up all my things and leave. Start again. I'd thought about it often over the last couple of months. I'd thought about moving to Scarborough, a nearby town, but it was a scary thing for a young woman just to pick up and move to a new place without any support. I sat there, utterly defeated, afraid for my safety, wondering whether Neil was going to come and attack me. The situation now was ten times worse than it had been yesterday. And my Dad hadn't come back and seen the window. I couldn't listen to anyone and Jane just sat staring at me.

Jane and Scott were talking between themselves about my Dad. What I hadn't realised until that day, was that they had a strange kind of respect for each other. They were on each other's level, one that I had never been on with either of them. Scott's intentions all morning had been to get an argument flowing with my father. He was now continuing that hostility towards my father with Jane.

That's when a different kind of danger became apparent and it was one which my mind was not ready or equipped to deal with, following the morning's events. I needed to go somewhere, anywhere but here, to feel safe and try to clear my mind. Jane looked over to me harshly, after she had listened to Scott's resentment for my father.

"Why don't you get your Dad beaten up?" she suggested, as if it was the most obvious thing in the world. "I know loads of people who can do it."

I looked at her in total disbelief, still trying to deal with the disappointment of my behaviour that morning.

"No," I replied forcefully, my thoughts snapping back into the room. "Don't be stupid. I don't want my father beaten up."

I could think of nothing worse than knowing that my father was being beaten.

"Why," she said scornfully, as if I was being unreasonable. I had to explain to her, in simple terms, why a daughter wouldn't want that.

"Just because I couldn't bear to sit at home thinking of him getting beaten."

My head started buzzing, I realised that I was in more danger than I thought. Something was in the air here. Scott and Jane were clearly communicating something to each other, making eye contact knowingly with one another. I feared for my safety, this woman could have me beaten up too, if she knew that kind of people. She had visited me in my home recently, demanding to know why I hadn't been seeing her and trying to force me to be her friend. Just like Scott, she knew that I had rejected her. She had warned me that I should be more careful. It was only a couple of weeks before that she was venting about another woman she hated, spouting her venomous plans for revenge on that woman. It was this that had made me want to stay away from her again.

"I've paid someone to give that fucking bitch a scar on her face," she'd told me. "Who does she think she is marrying Adam?" I had no idea if it was true or not, but those words had set alarm bells ringing and after that, I had stayed away from her.

"Who do you think you are; do you think you're too good for me?" There it was again, that same accusation. I didn't want to hear it. I just wanted to go home.

"I'll do it," Scott burst out, referring to beating up my Dad. He was eager to please her. The day was becoming more surreal with every passing minute.

"You can do it?" she said. It sounded rehearsed, fake, as if it had been said before. Jane looked at my stunned face. It was like she was thriving on my fear.

"Yes, I can do it, I've done it before. I've killed people," he boasted.

"Killed people?" Jane repeated. She looked impressed and glanced over to me again, watching my reaction. I could hardly breathe. She grinned.

"Yes," he reiterated slowly, as if to drive the words home. "I have killed people."

He didn't even look my way; it wasn't me he was trying to impress, it was Jane. Jane looked thrilled, her face alive with excitement.

"I've stabbed someone," he said, standing up and making stabbing movements into the air.

"Who did you kill?" I said, weakly. I was no longer masking my emotions; I was terrified and I was transparent. After this horrible day was over, I was never going to see them again. I knew that for sure, even if I had to leave my home. I wanted the name of the victim, to be able to go to the police. Without it, I knew I would not be believed. They both looked at me, knowing that I would have gone to the police, and ignored me.

"Come on Scott," Jane said and they disappeared into the kitchen.

My brain was overloaded with shock from one danger after another and my thoughts suddenly came all at once; *go to the police ... they will kill you ... they will deny what you're saying ... The police have done nothing to help you ... why would they help you now ... and then you will be in danger from them both ... you've heard what they are capable of ... Get all your family together and don't let them out of your sight.*

Solutions, followed by all the reasons they wouldn't work, fired rapidly through my mind. It was hopeless. At the same time, my rational mind argued for common sense; they're *not going to do anything ...* I argued with myself about the level of danger I was really in, or should I say my father, or both of us? It was surreal and impossible, if I could just get this one day out of the way, I could pack up and leave forever.

Jane came out of the kitchen and picked up a map. "Michelle has to be there," she said to Scott, looking straight at me. I sat powerless and isolated in Jane's armchair, next to the TV, which was now blaring in my ear. I hadn't realised it then, but I had sunk into some sort of dazed state. I couldn't hear anything of what they were saying. I was immobilised with not only one psychopath, but two. If I ever get out of today, I told myself, I would never return to this house again. In full discussion, they left the house.

"Don't you go anywhere, I won't be long." Jane locked the door as she and Scott left and, as she'd said, she was back soon enough, maybe it was ten minutes. During that time, I longed for my father. I looked out of the window to see both him and Lewis return and wanted to bang on the window. I didn't. He was drunk, illogical and would be angry with me. His long auburn hair swayed in the air and it made me miss him terribly. I'm going to make up with him as soon as I get out of this house.

"You look afraid," Jane sneered, when she got back. I said nothing. I didn't ask where she had been or where Scott was or what they were saying in the kitchen earlier. I knew it was bad, as I had heard what they were saying before they went in.

"I am going to make up with my Dad," I told her, trying to take back some small piece of control.

"Are you?" she said in a high-pitched voice "How are you going to go over there, when Neil wants to kill you? Bring him over here."

I was trying to appease everyone in several situations at once and my Dad was happy to get out of the house and speak to me at Jane's. Even though I heard what she had said earlier, I still complied. That's who I was. Of course, he forgave me for everything. I returned the presents I had taken and I told him I was sorry. When I picked my daughter up from school that afternoon, I bought him a bottle of whiskey to make up. But Jane had come to the school with me and insisted I return to her house. "Just wait until Scott comes back, he can take you home".

I was hoping that what I had heard was perhaps all talk and nothing was going to happen to my father – perhaps it was over, as Jane was happily chatting away with my Dad – I couldn't make sense of any of it any more. But just to be sure, I tried to get my whole family, even Neil, under the one roof, by inviting them all to tea. It didn't work – in the end only my mother came.

Scott had returned and taken over Jane's domineering presence. He took my mum and me home. I didn't say anything to my mother about what I had heard. How could I? Given her mental health, I had no idea what that information might do to her. And here I was, worrying that something may or may not happen to my father. My fear of Scott had increased after realising that he may be capable of killing someone. I had no idea if any of it was real. All I had heard was that Scott had offered to beat up my Dad and that he had killed someone before. There was nowhere else to go that night – I was trapped in my own mind, going round in circles.

He was walking around my house like he owned the place. My mum seemed oblivious and was happily watching the TV; she didn't even notice.

"Get changed," he said, throwing me some clothes. My mother looked confused.

"Are you going out?"

"I don't know," I told her.

"Awwe, that's nice, go out." She seemed pleased that he and I were getting on, as she saw it, the momentary discomfort of a few weeks ago, when Scott had followed my dad, already forgotten. Although I didn't comply with the change of clothes, I left the house with him ten minutes later. I went out with him, not only because my mother had encouraged me, but also to see where he was going and to ensure my Dad was safe from him.

He drove us straight to my Dad's. As soon as I walked into the house, Neil literally wanted to kill me; he had to be restrained and Dad and Scott took him upstairs.

It was obvious to me that Scott was angry with my father that night. I could hear it in the tone of his voice every time he addressed him. No one else noticed it, they were all too drunk and he kept the glasses topped up with cider. When that was gone, he got the bottle of whiskey that I had bought earlier for my dad out of the cupboard. He kept asking my Dad to go to Jane's and I realised that my time was running out. Perhaps it was possible he would hurt my father after all, and on this night.

My moment was coming that I would do something to protect him. "He is a nice bloke, that Scott," Lewis said, when they were all upstairs trying to stop my brother from attacking me. "You should treat him right. He was that angry with you the other day, he was planning to petrol bomb your house."

I looked at Lewis, not with contempt, knowing that he was trying to scare me, but as a potential helper for me and for my Dad's safety. I looked at him, weighing up his likelihood of success in that role, as not only my father's life depended upon it, but mine also. I had the opportunity right there and then to ask him to help. This man despised me that much, there was the possibility he wouldn't. I didn't risk it and at that moment, when Scott and my father came downstairs, I plucked up my courage to try to get help elsewhere. There was still hope.

"Me and Lewis have been talking about rune stones."

We had, at one point. He told me that he had had them read. I said I was going to see Donna and Ben, they had some and Lewis and I wanted to have a go. Lewis nodded, unfamiliar with me offering to do things with him. It was unusual for me to talk to him so much and without contempt, however, I was desperate now for an ally. Scott glared at me as if to say, *don't you move.* I headed to the door. There was absolutely nothing that Scott could do. It had been the only thing I could think of. Donna and Ben lived as close to my Dad as Jane, but in the opposite direction. They were strong, streetwise people. They would know what to do. As soon as the door shut behind me, I ran. I ran so fast that I bumped into my Dad's next door neighbours, coming through my father's front yard. My watch dropped from my wrist as I bumped into them with my arm.

"Oh dear," they said. I nearly asked them to help me to get help.

But as I looked at their faces, I knew that they were sick of the noise and they had threatened to report him to the council in the last week.

"I'm OK," I panicked and ran past them.

I couldn't believe it when I got to Donna and Ben's house. They were a sure thing of being in. Donna and Ben were always in, but tonight, all the lights were off. I knocked on the living room window, like I always had. They had been in trouble with the police lately and I didn't know whether they were out, or pretending not to be in. I frantically looked about. There was no one else I knew in this area. I only knew them as friends of my father's. My chance was gone. My mind scrambled for another solution. I had to get back to Scott without him guessing I was planning to reveal his plot. *It's not really going to happen,* I tried to convince myself. I still couldn't believe it. I was stuck in a nightmare. I walked back into the house. Scott looked like I had got one over on him and he was not happy. It was a risk I had to take. He went to see Neil upstairs, to care for him again.

Time was getting on and I asked Scott to take me home. He stared at me with contempt. Lewis nearly choked with laughter as he watched the young woman, who made a constant judgement about him, being put in her place. I tried another tactic, claiming that I needed to go to the shops.

"Get me some cigarettes papers if you're going," Lewis asked, giving us a reason to come back. Lewis had ruined my plans. I had to get Scott away from my father and then I would get away from him. I had no idea of any details of Jane and Scott's plans, where or how, or even if they had a plan at all. I didn't know what to do. I was winging it from moment to moment trying to think of the next thing to do, to avoid my father from being beaten or even worse, killed. I tried to be civil.

"Look, I'm really tired," I told him at the shop. "I just want to go home." He didn't say anything to me, maintaining a stony faced silence. The night was long and he continued to ignore my pleas. Before long, he was encouraging my Dad to go to Jane's again. Knowing this was his chance to get my Dad alone, I invited Lewis too.

"I'm not going to that bitch's house," Lewis said. "She stitched me up for a crime; I fucking hate her guts."

"We can't leave Lewis here on his own," I said, giving another reason not to go. Scott convinced my Dad to get his coat on, with a promise of plenty of weed to be smoked.

"It's OK," Lewis was being reasonable. "I'll wait for him." I started walking with them across to the gate, when Scott hesitated.

"I won't be a minute ... keep going," he told me. I'd only got to the corner of the street before I started to encourage my father to go home. After that, I would be able to go home myself, my father would be safe for another day and then I would be able to put some safety measures in place for us all.

"She's not in, Dad."

"What?" he said, disappointedly.

"She is not in, Dad, the lights are off. Let's get you home." As we were walking back, Scott pulled up in a car, but not the car he drove most of the time, that car was still parked outside of Jane's. I was confused. Looking back, it must have been placed on my father's street all day, even though I hadn't seen it there. If he had not wanted to trick either my Dad or myself, Scott would have just taken us to the car on Jane's street.

I knew this other car. He had let me drive in the couple of days that I was complying with him. Seeing him in it in these circumstances threw me.

"Where are you going?" He was clearly angry,

"I am taking Dad home," I replied. "Jane's not in." I didn't care if she was in or not, I just wanted my Dad to believe the lights were off.

"Get in the car, I'm going to the garage."

It was then that I hesitated. My Dad was turned around, going back home and I could have carried on walking from there and ignored Scott. But I didn't. I hesitated for that one second and faltered, not knowing what to do or say.

"I'm getting some tobacco, I've run out. I'll get you some, Keith." With that, my Dad was happy to get in the car and that's when I crawled into the back of the small, two-door car and my Dad got into the front.

I have analysed that moment over and over again. In my heart, I did not want anything to happen to my Dad. I don't know why I made myself and my father become vulnerable at that moment. It was at that point I lost my father and myself as I was and there was no way out. This is the nightmare that I have never been able to wake up from.

Chapter 15

Scott turned the car the wrong way from the garage; left into the dark roads, instead of right into the well-lit streets. I felt myself shrinking into the back of the car, becoming smaller and smaller by the second. The events of the day had totally overwhelmed me. I could barely function.

Scott stared straight ahead into the road whilst he was driving. He seemed fixated not just on the road, but in his mind, as I'd seen him do so many times in the last six weeks. He didn't speak at all, to either my father or myself, for what seemed an eternity. Scott and my father shared not only the bottle of whiskey together, but also a bottle of wine. Scott had a number of joints already rolled in the front of the car; had they been prepared earlier for this moment? I felt that Scott was using everything, including the bottle of whiskey I had bought earlier, to get my dad intoxicated. Scott appeared to be drinking straight from the bottle as he drove. I felt as though he was only pretending to drink before passing the bottle over to my father to copy him.

All I could hear in the car was the music that was playing. I have never been able to listen to it again, to this day. It was one of my favourite artists at the time, but since that day, it only triggers a memory of horror. *M People,* blaring out of the speakers into the back of the car, that song now imprints on my mind with my emotions of horror.

I looked behind me helplessly and saw a car behind us. Someone so close behind might be able to get help, if I could alert them to our danger. Could I wave to them without Scott seeing? I could even perhaps write 'help' on the back window, in the steam and smoke that had misted up from our breaths and the joints. It was a ridiculous thought and my mind argued back. *He will see you. You could be killed.* I looked on the floor in front of me. The floor was covered with all sorts of things. I tried to look down, perhaps to find something which I could pick up without being seen, so that I could hit Scott on the back of his head. Even looking down to the floor caused me great terror and he had even noticed that. Every bit of my behaviour was being watched. Even though there was only one of him, but two of my Dad and me, I felt we were both vulnerable and that he was a force to be reckoned with. I felt an empty bottle with my foot.

"What are you doing," he barked, as I used my foot to kick around the rubbish in the back of the car.

"Nothing," I replied, as calmly as I could. I was trying to appear compliant to his wishes, whatever they were.

"I was just wondering if you had a bottle of wine in the back of the car." It was all I could think of. He passed me the bottle of wine and, like him, I pretended to drink it. He glared at me in the mirror. I nearly put myself in danger ... even if I did hit him I would have to knock him out to be out of danger ... and then the car would go out of control and we would all be killed. Just like earlier in the day, my mind had good reasons why all of my solutions would not work.

After about ten or fifteen minutes, even though alcohol was being passed around, apart from the music there was an eerie silence. My father broke it, like a peacemaker, asking as a joke where we were going. He wasn't confrontational. Neither of us was.

"OK," he said, the teasing note in his voice sounding forced. "Where are you taking me?"

Did he know he was in danger?

"I've got you a woman." Scott appeared completely in control; I had to lean forward to hear what they were saying. It was easy for him to just roll off lies, he had done it lots of times by now. Now, in the car, he painted a scenario of a potential date for my father. I dared to butt into the conversation.

"It's a little late, Dad. Perhaps, if you want to see her, you might want to go on another day, at a reasonable time." Time, though, in my father's world, pretty much went around a twenty-four-hour clock and it seems he hadn't had a girlfriend now for sixteen years; it's not difficult to imagine how and why he took the bait.

"No," my father said, "I want to go." Scott took his eyes off the road and stared at me both in the mirror and by turning around. He was ordering me to shut up, without speaking a single word. It was obvious he hated me.

He lit another joint and passed it over to my father. He was using all of them to get him more intoxicated, it was clear.

I had absolutely idea of where we were going. I saw a red telephone box and wished I could call someone for help. The car journey seemed to take hours. I had lost all concepts of time and instead felt only mounting terror. It was as if time had stopped altogether. We passed a sign saying Kirbymoorside and then one saying Helmsley.

The car started slowing down. The road beneath felt like track; bumpy and gravelly. I felt like we were on this road, or roads like it, for at least another hour, it was only the change in road surface that brought a sense of time back into my consciousness. He stopped the car near a gate and asked my father, who was now nearly asleep in the car, to get out. He didn't. Scott asked him again. He didn't move.

"He doesn't want to get out of the car," I told him. My father looked around at me for some kind of understanding of what was going on. In that moment, we recognised that both of us had fear in our eyes. I wished I could have told him he was in danger. He was a small built man, only five foot seven and he was intoxicated. Even if I had told him he was in danger, Scott could have easily have hit him one time to knock him unconscious and leave me stuck in the back of the car to face him alone. I couldn't give him any reason to do that.

"Get changed," Scott ordered me, breaking the unspoken communication between my father and me. I looked at him, confused and wary.

"Get changed," he said again. I complied, not with fear but with abject terror. My mind had long since passed understanding any logic … I thought he might kill me. He pointed to a carrier bag already prepared on the back seat. I got changed in the back of the car with Scott watching me in the wing mirror. My Dad didn't turn around. Scott drove the car again, past the gate, before stopping on a track near a field. In that moment, I had a flash of realisation of the enormity of the danger we were in. Although I was terrified, my mind still could not allow it. He stopped the car, leaving the headlights on, went to the back of the car and took some items out of the boot. I hadn't known there was anything in the boot.

Think Michelle, think! Terror and confusion engulfed me, my options to find a way out were now even more limited. Had he left the keys in the ignition? I am almost certain I would have driven the car away, leaving him there in the middle of nowhere, if he had. They were gone. He had taken them out, to either unlock the boot, or to prevent me from driving the car. Even the thought of driving away caused my mind to panic. I thought about how long we had driven over the bumpy, off road tracks and how slowly I would have had to have driven, not knowing the way back to a main road. I would then have to make it home before he did, in case he killed my family. It didn't even occur to me that he would have had no way of getting home. All of my focus was encompassed by fear.

The passenger side door opened from the outside, within a couple of minutes. He reached in to get my father out of the car. He was a large man compared to my father and pulled him out of the car with ease. He walked him a couple of metres into the field. I watched in horror from the back of the car as my father fell and Scott started dragging him onto the field. I had to do something to stop it – I didn't know what to do. I scrambled out of the back seat of the car and followed them onto the field.

He was hitting my father, with what I thought was a baseball bat, up and down his body. All I could do was to cover my eyes like a young child, feeling too small to do anything. He said nothing, he just kept hitting and hitting, his face chillingly calm.

I looked on the floor, there were other tools there. Could I pick one up and hit him, if he had his back to me for at least thirty seconds? *You're going to have to knock him out with one blow*, I told myself. What if I didn't, though? I was terrified. He could have killed me with just one of his blows. Selfishly, I feared for my own life.

Abruptly he stopped hitting and walked calmly back to the car

Was he going to drive away and leave us there, or he was coming back? I scurried to my father's side and looked around for a way to escape. There was a boulder … perhaps if I got my father to it, we could hide. I also saw a house with a light on in the distance. Deep down, I knew I wasn't going to make it to either of those places. I looked up at the sky and said out loud.

"Help me, God, please help me."

Scott walked back calmly towards us. He was in no hurry.

"Move!"

I moved away slightly from my father. Scott started to pour liquid from a red container. The stench of petrol filled my nostrils.

"What are you doing? What are you doing?" I cried over and over again. Was it the smell or the pouring of the liquid that penetrated the shock? For the first time that day, I suddenly realised it was all real. I knew, then, that my father was going to be killed.

I just started to run, like I did when I was a child, running away. I got half way to the car and the whole field lit up. I turned around instantly, running to my father to save him. In that moment, my mind could only see a fire burning rubbish.

"That's not my Dad! That's not my Dad!" I screamed over and over again. Scott didn't even look at me. He was busy picking up all the things he had taken out there with him to the moor. I ran straight to my father and what I saw then was an image that I will never be able to remove from my mind. At that moment, I died out there with him. My father was gone, and inside, I was dead.

Scott shouted for me to get back in the car.

Over the years I have replayed that night over and over again. Sometimes, in the wish to clear my name, I've wished I were killed too, at least in an attempt to prevent my father from being killed, which I know would have happened. At least then, I would have kept my dignity and integrity, something which I have never been able to gain back, and nor will gain back, should I ever clear my name. But no, there was another plan for me, one that was to be revealed in the next couple of hours and days.

The night still wasn't over. Even though I was suffering the deepest trauma, I was still able to realise it had only just begun. On that long drive back to Bridlington, my senses struggled to make sense of an unreal situation. The Michelle that once was, was now left in the dark moor with her father, still looking for hope. When I got back into the car, the front seat was still in the forward position, where I had put it to get out and try and stop the attack from happening. It represented failure now and would be a feeling that would eat away at me for many years to come. I held onto that seat to steady myself getting into the back of the car. I was leaving without my father; my father who had protected me and whom I had failed to protect. I sat for the duration of the journey in silence. It was not over. Scott was not only still in my life; he had destroyed it completely. Near the end of the journey he told me to hand over the clothes I was wearing. I changed back into the clothes I had worn earlier, placed the clothes he had brought back into the carrier bag and handed them over to him. I didn't ask why. There was no fight left inside me. He looked calm, almost peaceful.

I still realised that my life depended on how and what I did from now on. I had seen him murder my father, he didn't need to threaten me; I complied out of fear.

I had no idea of why Scott pulled up outside Jane's. He instructed me with the story I was to tell.

"When you get home, I want you to tell people that you have had had a change of heart," he said, without even looking at me. "Tell them you have now realised you love me and that we are going to be married."

The fight inside of me was gone and I just nodded my head. Only yesterday, there was hope.

I sat in the car, not knowing what he wanted me to do.

"Get out" he said, coldly, "We're going into Jane's."

Jane opened the door, looking frustrated with Scott. She didn't even look at me, she just moved out of the way to let me pass, as if my movements were already decided.

"Where the hell have you been? I've had to end up going to bed and Greg is here, so you need to be quiet … don't you dare wake him up."

"I couldn't find the place you said," Scott told her, his voice low.

"Where the hell did you go then?" she asked him. "Never mind that now, just take the stuff to the place where we agreed." She stopped talking and looked at me.

"Go in the living room," she ordered. Their voices in the hallway were quiet now and I couldn't hear what they were saying, but I'd heard enough to understand they were setting me up for the murder of my own father. Of course, I would be the prime suspect from the argument they had caused and escalated in the morning. Scott, it seemed, was now going to bury my clothes along with the weapons in a place unknown to me. I had no idea where at the time, but I overheard, a couple of days later, during an argument between them, that perhaps they might be at Woldgate, a small wooded location on the outskirts of Bridlington.

When Jane came in, she sat across from me, leaning forward with an expression I could not read.

"How does it feel to watch your Dad being killed?" She peered at my face, blowing smoke into it. I didn't and couldn't answer her. I sat in silence, shell-shocked.

"You're not too good for me now," she mused.

She was right. When the police arrested me a week later, Jane would become the main witness against me.

When Scott returned, he handed me the keys to the car in which he'd driven my father to his murder and told me to drive it home. He was going to remove the car he usually drove, which had been left outside Jane's all night. The idea of them setting me up to drive the car he had taken my father in was only a distant thought. I had more important things to worry about; my daughter and my mother. I drove as quickly as I could to my home. I tried to get there before he did. My mind was focused on survival from minute to minute. It didn't dawn on me then that he would have had to have planted the car I was now driving on my Dad's road early in the afternoon, along with the tools, leaving his own car parked outside Jane's all night, perhaps as an alibi. Perhaps that's what he and Jane had done when they locked me in her house that afternoon. It was a car he had allowed me to drive for a couple of days previously. I sped back home, thinking I could have made it there before him, but he pulled up seconds later in the car park, just as I was getting out.

Scott followed me closely into *my* house. I was still shell shocked. The turning of the key in the back door awoke my mother and she shouted to me as we walked up the stairs.

"I've been worried about you," she said. It was now the early hours of the morning.

"Tell your mum the good news," he urged, lingering at the room where my mum was awake in bed and my daughter slept. I could have cried out loud if this had been a normal trauma of a sudden death or the news of an accident. This trauma was continuing and watching my mum whole heartedly smile at him made her suddenly appear vulnerable and not the threatening figure she had represented so many times in my younger years. I wanted to hug her and protect her and my daughter. I complied with his wishes, not knowing what he would do next, knowing only that this was a mad man who had gone completely off the rails.

"Awwe, lovely!" she cooed. "At last!" She liked him and agreed with him that I had finally come to my senses.

"I thought you said you didn't like him and you were getting him out of your house," my mum commented, when I got into bed with her and my daughter. That moment, in bed with my mum and my daughter, was the first time that day that I was alone from either Scott or Jane. It didn't seem to make sense, even to her, that I left her house only twenty-four hours earlier with frustrated demands to get him out. The house was small. "Mum," I whispered.

"What's up?" she bellowed, in her loud Liverpool accent. He would definitely have heard her. All the doors to the bedrooms were open and it was a small, two bedroomed, terraced house.

"Night, Mum," I answered, with a final sense of loss. He was in the next bedroom and he might overhear anything I said. I said nothing at all. I was frozen. I looked at my daughter in the dark bedroom, overwhelmed by the need to protect both her and my mother. I lay in bed suffering from intense shock and trauma. Every second was slowed down in my brain. I lay there with my eyes wide open, staring into the blackness all night, but instead of seeing a black room, all I could see was my father's burning body.

My mother peered into my face with uncharacteristic concern the following morning. She told me that I didn't look well at all and offered to take my daughter to school. I was left to lie in my bed, vacant and dead, unable to function.

"Don't worry, Michelle, I'll pick your daughter up for you. I hope you get better soon." My mother hadn't been gone long, before he shouted me downstairs. When I got there, he was standing in the kitchen, near the door.

"Look in here," he said, holding a cup in his hand. He shoved it at my face ... "It's a spider," he shouted. I had no choice but to look, but there was no spider. At the bottom of the cup were the remains of a biscuit, but no spider. I looked at him. By now, I expected no sense from this strange and dangerous man. I felt as though he was trying to make me question my sanity and logic. That's when part of the shock loosened on my frozen body and I vomited on the way to the toilet upstairs.

What happened over the next few days was a blur. I seemed to lose a sense of my surroundings, swamped by feelings of numbness and detachment. It was like I was being sucked into a big black hole and the whole time, either Jane or Scott was constantly at my side. That evening, my mother came to inform me she hadn't seen my father that day. Of course, I wanted to tell my mother he was dead. More than anything, I wanted my father to be found. I couldn't bear the thought of his body laying out in the middle of nowhere, cold, on that desolate moor. My mother asked if I had seen him. I told her the last time I saw my father was at the garage, the night before. I hadn't seen him after that, I lied. Scott hadn't told me what to say, but I just told the closest to the truth that I could.

"What is wrong with you, Michelle?" my mother kept asking, putting my shock down to some sort of virus. Each time I closed my eyes, I could see my father being killed. As if that wasn't horrific enough, the killer was still in my house with me and had I said anything, he might kill me and my family as well.

The plan unfolded. "I think we both know what's best for you," he said, on the Friday night. I knew he was suggesting that I should commit suicide. My life was over and I knew it. In the depths of trauma and despair, I agreed that that was for the best.

"It's for the best," he repeated. "I'll help you do it."

I nodded in agreement, so completely detached from reality, I was easily going along with his plan. If it had gone according to plan, the truth of this story would never have been told. The prime suspect would, herself, be dead, no more questions asked. Scott's obsession had completely shifted to my brother, had he succeeded, perhaps he would have had my brother for himself?

Jane came to the house regularly over the next couple of days. She sat and watched me staring into space. I had given up.

On the Sunday night, only two days after the murder, I convinced Scott to let me out of the house. He was reluctant at first. A voice was beginning to stir deep inside of me. *Fight!* It was quiet, but I heard it.

"I just need some women's things," I told him.

"I'm timing you." The threat was clear. He gave me the keys to his car. I drove to a phone box a few streets away. Panicking, I picked up the receiver to call Mickey, my father's and brother's closest friend. Scott had given me ten minutes. The phone didn't work. I could hardly breathe. As fast as I could, I got back into the car. I had to drive a mile to the next phone box and go to the shop all within ten minutes. Hyper-ventilating. I reached the phone box and dialled the number.

"Answer! Answer!" I prayed out loud. A woman answered the phone.

"Hello," It was Mickey's girlfriend, Katty.

"Katty," I gasped. "It's Michelle, is Mickey there?"

"No, Michelle he's out, you'll have to call back later."

"Katty, no!" I pleaded, before she had a chance to put down the phone. "I need Mickey to come around tonight, its urgent, it's an emergency, it's about Dad."

"Ok, Michelle I'll let him know. What's up with him.?"

"He has gone missing." I had to go along with what everyone thought. I couldn't tell her the truth; I hardly knew her. Mickey was my only hope; he had been like a brother to me. He could protect me and help me go to the police in safety.

Please, Katty," I begged again. "Please tell him to come around tonight. I don't care if it's in the middle of the night, I need his help."

"OK, Michelle, bye." I got in the car. I had been gone too long. I drove back to a place I could no longer call my home.

"You've been gone more than fifteen minutes," he said, drawing himself up to his full height. I didn't care now. I knew it wouldn't be long, there was hope that Mickey would be able to save me. He would help us all get safely away from Scott, so that we could go to the police. I went to bed that night with a glimmer of hope for escape.

I stayed awake most of that night, waiting for Mickey to come. It was a crushing blow when I finally realised that he wasn't going to turn up. My desperate attempt to get help had failed again.

"I know you're up to something," Scott growled the next day.

"I will kill you, Michelle, if I even think you will tell anyone. I will also kill the rest of your family, your mum and your daughter. If I'm caught, I will kill the police and if I go to prison I will kill the officers too. There is no one I won't kill. I know people I can go to get guns." He went on to mention someone by the name of Irish John. I believed him.

Mickey finally arrived on the Monday afternoon in response to the message I had left the previous night. The room was full when he arrived. He gently asked me if I had any idea where my father could have been. I changed my story. Of course I did. I wasn't rehearsed, like Scott or Jane, and the last thing in my mind was to keep a story straight. I was more concerned with keeping me and my family safe and seeking help.

"Who saw him last?" Mickey asked.

"My brother, I think."

"I thought you said it was you?" My mother looked confused.

"Come on," Mickey encouraged me, "we'll go out and look for him. He didn't ask my brother or my mother to go with him. He knew if anyone was to look day or night for him, that person was me.

Scott lifted my daughter and placed her on his knee. My daughter looked at me for reassurance.

"Remember," he said, "Your mum and your daughter are here."

I knew there was nothing I could do. He had my family and I had no doubt, whatsoever, that he would carry out his threats if I crossed him.

"Where do you think he could be?" Mickey asked, in this car.

At any other time, only I would have known where he would be. I knew my father like no one else. Mickey went to a couple of people's houses and I went along with him, not doing or saying anything. Mickey told me to go into various places, saying it was better coming from me, as his daughter. Half an hour later, I sat in his car, staring into space, not even answering him, feeling that I couldn't even speak any longer.

"It's OK, Michelle," he said, comfortingly. He knew how much my father meant to me. He had known us all our life and had visited often when I lived with my father. We had sat for hours and talked when I was younger; we had shared our lives' ambitions and dreams together. He had once asked me if I would ever move out of Bridlington, or would I stay in this small town forever?

"I could never leave my father," I had told him. All he thought of today was comforting me and promising me he was going to bring my Dad back. I knew that wasn't possible and I sat in the front of his car looking straight ahead. We sat on the eastern road estate, a part of my mind willing me to tell him what had happened. If anyone can help me, Mickey can help me. I could feel the words rising up in my throat. I could hear them in my brain saying, *Mickey help me.* Just then, Stuart, a friend of Mickey's, who had come to help search for my dad, walked over to the car and started talking to Mickey. It was too late. Not even Mickey could save me. Mickey looked concerned, but was in a rush to drop me off. He had somewhere else to go. He seemed puzzled when I hesitated to get out of his car.

"We will find him for you," he promised and kissed me.

My hope, raised again for such a short time, was gone. I stood on the path outside my house, watching him drive off.

I went inside, wondering if Scott had worked out that I must somehow have contacted Mickey for him to have turned up like that. When everyone had left, he told me of the plans for my suicide.

"You can drive the car over the cliffs," he said. "Or just jump off. Write a suicide note. I'll help you."

I nodded, ready to give in again. Out of the blue, for the first time, he offered me some kind of explanation.

"I know how terrified you were ... and are," he said, before trying to shift the blame away from himself.

"Jane told me she gets a thrill from scaring you, she finds it funny," he went on, "She told me that you're scared of her and that you were abused by your father."

Tears were now streaming down my face. He went on to talk about the drugs and Neil.

"I didn't blame my Dad for that," I cried, "I blamed Lewis."

He was completely insane. Somehow, he thought, in his crazy world, that avenging what he believed to have been my father's abuse of me (even though it had never happened) and what he saw as my father' responsibility for Neil's drug use were somehow explained in terms of Jane getting a kick out of scaring me. That was it? That was his explanation?

"I'll kill Lewis then, to make up."

"Stop it." I said. "I can't hear anymore." How could anything make up for what he had done to my father?

He made himself a cup of tea and pottered around the house, just like it was a normal day. A moment ago, I had wanted to give up. Now, listening to his rapidly unravelling sanity, I knew I had to find a way out.

I had a sudden flash of clarity. In his madness, if I could get him to believe I was on his side, playing along, I might be able to get away and get help properly. I started to speak to him; I needed him to trust me.

The plot had started to become frighteningly clear. Jane and Scott, both rejected by, me, were equally as revengeful as each other. Scott had become obsessed with my brother, my family and me. He clearly had serious emotional and mental difficulties. If I had been abused, in his mad understanding, I would have some kind of motive to have my dad "punished." My clothes and the weapons had been taken somewhere – I didn't know where. A car I had used before had been used for the murder, I had driven it back to my house that night. Whilst we were on the moor, Scott had left his car outside of Jane's all night.

I was implicated every step of the way, even though I had nothing to do with any of it. The pieces were starting to fit together – all of the manipulation and control had been designed to point the finger at me.

The plan next was for me to commit suicide. It would then be finished – the explanation would be that I'd killed myself in remorse for what I'd done to my father, and no further questions would be asked.

Was this just a game to them? Some sort of sick, vengeful, spiteful scheme, giving each of them some warped satisfaction? None of it made any sense, even as I began to fit all the pieces together.

He was visiting Mark on the Monday night. My family were all at my house that evening, but I was to go with him. It was supposed to be a short visit, but I prolonged the conversation; I felt a sense of safety with Mark, perhaps because he had confided previously in me that he, himself, thought Scott to be strange. Could I find a way to tell him what had happened?

After a couple of drinks, Scott wanted to go to the shop. He didn't leave me anywhere on my own, so I had to go in the car with him. I jumped out of the car into the street on our way back to Mark's. The glass of wine I'd had earlier had given me courage. I started to knock on people's doors, but nobody answered. I ran to a man, a total stranger on the street, and asked him to help me. He looked at me like I was crazy. The truth was, at that point, I probably was. Desperate to get away from Scott, I hid down an alley. He parked the car at the exit.

"Get back in the car, Michelle," he commanded, darkly.

I had run down a dead end, there was nowhere to go. Driving back to Mark's house again, I could feel Scott's fury.

"I told you, I'll kill you, Michelle, and your daughter."

Back at Mark's house, I accepted another glass of wine – I had taken a chance and there was no telling what Scott would do now.

Mark looked uncomfortable in his own home; it was late and he wanted to go to bed. We had nearly reached the car to go back to my house when the consequences of my earlier behaviour became clear. Scott was going to Jane, both of them would be sorting me and my family. I ran back to Marks and banged on his door.

"What the hell is going on?" he said, opening the door to us both.

"Please help me," I said, not caring that Scott was right behind me.

Mark looked like he didn't want to get involved, however he told Scott, "I don't know what's going on, but she's safe here, she can stay on the sofa."

"Scott killed my father!" The words tumbled out.

"What?" Mark gasped in disbelief.

I told him the whole story.

"He will come back with Jane," I warned him.

"Help me go to the police, let's go now," I pleaded.

Much to my surprise, Mark hesitated.

"Wait," he said. "I know Scott might be a psychopath, but I don't know what we should say about Jane. Let me think about it. For now, you're safe. Stay here Michelle. I'll help you get away from him. You and your daughter can stay here until you feel safe again."

He let me sleep in his bed. Later, he climbed in beside me, trying to be intimate. Rejection of men hadn't gone well before and Mark was all I had to help me, so I went along with it. I didn't speak out in case he turned against me and didn't help me.

"Let me think about going to the police," he said. "It's not that you shouldn't go to the police, I need to think about what you have said about Jane."

Jane and Scott turned up the next day to collect me, just as I had told Mark that they would. I went in the car with them. Mark was gone. We should have gone to the police together.

I saw him again over the next two days. On the Thursday, he came to make sure I was OK.

"We'll go to the police together," he promised. "Try to keep Jane out of it, then I'll support you and you can come and stay with me with your daughter until you feel safe again." Safety was promised in the small town on the condition that I kept Jane out of it. Not understanding the psychological condition of post traumatic stress disorder, safety at this point was crucial and I was driven to seek safety for the sake of my mental health. Scott had gone to get a shot gun since he said that Jane hadn't returned.

I thought he was doing his best to help me. He came with me to the phone box on the estate, the one I'd tried to use earlier. It still wasn't working.

"My aunt! She lives just here! I'll go there and call the police. I can't go on my own." It had become clear that Mark didn't really want to go to the police with me, after all. I pressed the buzzer.

"Come in!" my Dad's sister, called out.

"I'm not coming in," Mark muttered.

"Please?" I begged.

"No!" He was resolute. "Keep hold of my jacket and I will see you soon. Don't forget, don't say anything about Jane."

I promised. I had hope.

Chapter 16

A lady Police Constable arrived in a police van at my aunt's, shortly after my call. I went down to meet her, my aunt standing at the window, watching for them arriving. I finally felt safe, sitting beside the PC, as she drove to the police station, after what had been the longest six days of my life. Driving through the estate, I was flooded with relief to hear that my mother and daughter were being taken into safety. At that point, I was sure I hadn't done anything unlawful by knowing something *might* happen, but being too afraid and out of my depth to do anything about it. Not having anyone to turn to was not a crime, *was it?* I wasn't aware of the complex nature of law at that point and instead of having a legal advisor, the only person who had advised me, up until then, was Mark.

Mark was related to Jane and was an ex-boyfriend of hers, something I hadn't thought about, as I clung to what I thought was his help, for dear life.

The police had done nothing to help me previously when Scott threatened us. I didn't believe they would have helped me on the day beforehand, when nothing had actually happened. *Would they have believed me?* It was easy to explain why I hadn't gone to the police in the first three days, I couldn't. The next three days, it was pressure and fear which stopped me, something which would later damage my defence catastrophically.

The PC, Marie, wrote things down on a piece of scrap paper and then asked me sign it, never once reminding me that these things may be used in evidence. It didn't matter; it was the truth, apart from the distance I had created surrounding Jane's part in things.

"She might be bad, Michelle, but she isn't that bad," Mark had told me. "It was Scott that killed your father, not her, after all."

I was convinced he was doing his best to help me and protect my family and what he said was true – it *was* Scott who had killed my father. I stuffed down the questions about whether he would have done so without Jane's involvement – my mind could not cope with any more. I was shocked beyond belief when Mark later denied saying those things.

"We're going to put you in a bed and breakfast," the PC told me, much later. "We need to keep you safe from Scott. We still haven't caught him and tomorrow, we will go and look for your father."

"Thank you," I told her, from the bottom of my heart. My Dad was going to be found and Scott was going to be arrested, we were all safe.

The room in the bed and breakfast was awful. The receptionist seemed to jump on me as I walked past her to go outside to use the phone.

"Michelle, are you OK?" she asked, her expression giving nothing away.

"Yes, thank you," I replied. "I'm just going out to use the phone." I just wanted to call Mark and let him know I was OK and to thank him again. The receptionist moved the phone towards me with a straight face, then smiled at me with her mouth, but not with her eyes. She was making it clear I was not to go outside.

The call rang out. I called again. No answer. It was strange. Mark didn't go out much. I later learnt that he stayed at Jane's all night, telling her and pre-warning her of what I had told him. He was supporting her not be caught up in a murder that I believed she had instigated.

I went back to my room and couldn't wait until the police officer returned, so I that I could feel safe again. I liked her. I trusted her. I was still experiencing hyper-vigilance and stared at the ceiling, unable to sleep, terrified that that Scott might find me. I must have finally dozed off, because I woke early, with a start. Hours before the police officer was due to arrive, I was seated in the reception area, waiting for safety.

Marie walked straight past me when she arrived.

"She never went out of the room," the receptionist told her. "She made one phone call."

"Who to?" I heard Marie ask. The receptionist directed Marie's attention to where I was sitting. She looked shocked, but covered it quickly with a kind smile. Was she protecting me, I wondered, or holding me captive? A new kind of confusion swept over me, but I still felt safe and held the police presence in high regard. They were the good people, after all.

"I am so sorry that I'm late, Michelle" Marie apologised as she came over to me.

"No problem," I reassured her and smiled at her with all my heart.

"We're going to look for your father," she said, in the car.

"I wanted to come to the police sooner," I told her, as we drove off.

"You're here, now," she reassured me. "You're going to be OK."

Throughout the car journey, I explained the whole story of trying to get help.

I had no idea where Scott had taken my father and me. I could only tell Marie what I knew.

"We went onto the Scarborough road after going to the shop," I said.

I recalled what I could from that terrible journey: the road signs Kirbymoorside, Helmsley, the telephone box at the side of the road. I described the changing ground beneath the tyres, although it was dark. I didn't tell her how hard it was when all I really remembered was that the night went on forever and the intense fear. I was focusing on finding my Dad. I wanted my Dad to be taken off the cold ground. I wanted his dead body to be safe.

It was a long day with Marie – we were still driving by the evening.

"What's going to happen if we can't find him?" I asked

"We're thinking of getting the helicopters in."

A short time later Marie told me that experts of the area had been called and she had relayed the information I had given her about the land.

I sat in the back of the car exhausted. I had not slept properly for days. I could not close my eyes without seeing, over and over again, my father being attacked.

A detective inspector sat in the front of the car with Marie whilst slumped in the back, by arm covering my eyes. The two officers began to talk – they must have thought I'd fallen asleep.

"What's going to happen to Michelle?"

"We would be using her as a witness if she was going to be dealt with in our area."

The detective inspector, I realised, was from a different police force. I didn't know, then, that the place my father had been killed could have an impact on where any future trial took place – at the time, it didn't matter, so long as Scott was held accountable for what he had done.

"A statement has already gone in about her," Marie continued. "A friend of hers."

That friend was Jane, who was to become the main prosecution witness.

"That's a shame," he said, getting out of the car. To this day, I don't know the man's name. All I know is that if I was to be dealt with in North Yorkshire, I would have been treated as a witness ... or would they have had to arrest me with the information Jane had brought to them? I knew nothing of the criminal justice system.

The detective inspector in charge of the case met us when we walked into the police station.

"Michelle Nicholson, I am a detective inspector. You obviously know PC Marie. You will also be aware that we have been conducting enquiries all day into the disappearance of your father. As a result of those and from what you have said, the body of a man has now been found on North Yorkshire Moors. I must caution you in relation to this. You do not have to say anything unless you wish to do so, but what you say may be given in evidence. I am arresting you for your involvement in the murder of Keith Nicholson."

Not only had I lost my father, I was being blamed for his death. I cried uncontrollably as I was taken to the charge desk. After being taken to a cell, a matron was called out to sit with me.

"I didn't do it," I sobbed. "I only knew Scott for six weeks; he is crazy."

A duty solicitor was called. I didn't have a solicitor. I hadn't really needed one before, despite Jane's intimidation of picking up a purse for her. Even then, I hadn't had a solicitor and the police had interviewed us together.

A solicitor from a firm in Hull spoke briefly to me. "I'll come back tomorrow," he promised.

I woke in the middle of the night, wanting to speak to my solicitor. I had lost all sense of time – all I needed now was someone to sort out this terrible mistake. The police officer dialled the number and held out the phone. No one answered, of course. I was taken back to my cell.

The matron assigned to sit with me got me a blanket. I thought I would die of shock and she sat up with me, comforting me. A doctor was called and prescribed diazepam for panic attack and shock.

"What is she doing with a blanket?" I heard an officer complain in the early hours of the morning. The matron was still in my cell – she had dozed off when the medication had finally pulled me into sleep. The officer in charge was not happy with her.

"This is a dangerous prisoner," he said.

The next day, another matron was sent to me. She asked me if I had been using drugs as she watched me vomit in the toilet, both before and in between police interviews. After the murder, I had lost a stone in weight – that was a lot for a person of my already tiny stature.

It was a different solicitor who arrived the next morning. I didn't feel as comfortable with him as I had felt with the previous solicitor, though I couldn't explain why.

"It's OK," he told me, "the other solicitor will pick up the work on Monday, he is just not here today."

In the first interview, I tried to explain some of the background. I wanted to give them a full account of what had happened. I had nothing to hide. I told them about the argument in the morning with my father and what had led to it. I didn't explain that Scott was not my boyfriend and that he had invaded my life.

When it came to Jane, I began to feel that the police were guiding me with specific questions. I was no longer able to tell them things as I experienced them.

"Just answer that you don't *know* what was said."

"We have spoken to Jane," they warned me, when I told the police about the horror of what I believed was her and Scott plotting against my father. I wished, more than anything, that I had fought back against Scott, not just to save my father's life, but also to be able to tell the police I had tried to stop it, even if that had meant risking my own life. Even though I didn't present myself always in the best light, I told them the truth. It was difficult, knowing there were three men in the interview room, two police officers and a duty solicitor. Although I believed the solicitor was supposed to be on my side, I didn't always feel supported. But I knew nothing of how these processes were conducted, and trusted that he was just doing his job. At times, I presented myself in a less than favourable way. They didn't have to pressure me. I was trying to be truthful. They were OK when I was telling them about the argument I had with my father and my brother. I didn't understand the hostility I could feel building in the room and I just wanted the interview to be over. The interviews started at 4 30 pm, just before tea and ended at 10 30 pm that night.

During one of the interviews, a police officer informed me that they had turned the witness Mark against me and he no longer believed my version. Back in the cell, I asked the solicitor if it was ok for the police to do that. He told me that it would go well for me.

After another interview, Martin, the DI in the case, brought in a new seal.

"We have damaged the seal on one of your tapes," he said. "Sign it again."

My solicitor said nothing. I didn't understand – I had been told at the beginning that the tapes should all be signed, in the room, in front of everyone. I signed the new seal, thinking at the back of my mind that this was not right.

The police also said, for the benefit of the tape, that I was nodding during interview, when I was clearly shaking my head. With so much important information to try to get across to them, I didn't question these comments. I didn't realise at the time that they could be in any way damaging.

I explained the whole story from the start to the end. The only thing I could not answer was what did Scott and Jane did with my clothes and the weapons. I told them that his clothes were with mine, but they were not. The only person who got changed that night, bizarrely, was me and I had handed my clothes to him.

I had told Marie, the PC, that he had killed someone before, I had heard him confess a week before, in Jane's living room. The hardest thing to explain was being in the same house with him and Jane at the time. I didn't know what they were doing. I believed they were plotting against my father and for some reason, wanted me to be there. I also knew they plotted to put my clothes and the weapons somewhere I did not know. They had created a situation which had become so complex, it had become impossible for me to provide a full explanation. I had an argument. I knew they were plotting something, but I was terrified so much that I could not function.

Before the last interview, my solicitor and the police went into another room. I was left in the interview room by myself. I could hear the debating. After what seemed a long time, they came back in. The leading Detective Inspector was no longer doing the questioning, the second officer in the room was.

"What did you do with the weapons?" he asked. "What did you do with your clothes?" The conversation with my solicitor, it seemed, had been decision time. They believed I was guilty. It felt as if this part, now, was just a process.

Later that night, I was in the charge room, being charged with murder. I could not bear to look at the word *murder* on the charge sheet, let alone understand how they thought I could murder my own father.

It was now Saturday the 18th September 1993. I would appear in court on Monday.

Chapter 17

I stood in the dock at the magistrate's court for the first time in Bridlington, looking up and recognising some of the many faces. One of my father's friends looked as shocked and as helpless as I did. There were friends there that I had known, some close and some acquaintances; all were very serious. I heard a bail plea but the prosecution stood up and I listened, again stunned, as the prosecution gave a believable story that I was in danger from my father's friends. They made my father sound like he was part of a circle of friends who used drugs and violence as a way of life. But the scene was set; my father was a drug addict and they were not going to give me bail, not only because of the seriousness of the crime, but for my own protection. Perspiration trickled down my face and the spinning in my head seemed to speed up – in the midst of the shock and disbelief, I noticed that my breathing had become shallow and my legs weak. Instead of listening to the magistrates, my focus had fixed on my body; that's all I can now remember. My next memories are of being laid down in the cells, being told I was going to prison.

Hours later, the van came to collect me.

A large, friendly sergeant told me, "You have a lot of support, you have had a fan club in the police reception."

He seemed like a strong and professional police officer whose words were empathic and without judgement. He was one of the first to speak to me in this way.

"Cover your head," he called, as I made my way to the van. When he was on duty during my short stay in the police cells, I heard him comment one day, "there is going to be no funny business on my shift". That night, I was given a blanket. I wondered what else he was suggesting he would stop from happening on his shift.

Another police officer, one of the local beat bobbies, came to the cells in support of me. He was a friendly beat bobby, the first time I met him, he was sitting in my father's house. He said he was just popping in to ask how people were and to get to know the local community. Any time I saw him, he always asked after my father and brother, he knew I was a Daddy's girl. Now, he said very little. Had he wanted to voice his support for me in front of the other police officers who, it seemed, were determined to ensure a conviction, officers who disbelieved me?

Coming out of the police station, the only person sitting outside, looking smug, was Jane. I cannot describe the look, but can only describe how I felt.

Stepping into the white secure van for the first time, I held onto a photo of my daughter, like a symbol that I would not be allowed to be taken away from her. I had never seen a van like this one, and just getting in was making me feel sick and claustrophobic. There were several small metal doors. Each mini-prison had a small metal seat and the 'room' was a metre width and length, if that. No seatbelts. I sat in the small metal enclosure. A woman shut the metal door and locked me in, looking at my face through the small plastic window in the door. I stared at my daughter's photo. She was beautiful. She had the happiest smile on her face – she was wearing at least eight necklaces made of multi coloured beads we had made together. It was taken only a couple of months ago. I wondered what she was feeling now.

I could barely see out of the plastic window. We drove past the estate where I lived with my daughter. Still in shock, the dreadful reality began to hit me. I was being taken away from my daughter, my home, my community, and my friends and … I was going to prison. That's when I retched. We were still in Bridlington, there were hundreds of miles to go and I was sick in my small compartment. I had dropped my photo and quickly tried to clean it up before the image faded. I felt so sad that even the photo I tried to cling to for hope had been partly damaged. It was all I had. The security woman put a plastic bag under the door. She also switched off the radio every time the news came on. There were some captors, it seemed, who held a kind of sensitivity for their prisoners. But, I had learned quickly, in my new social position of being a prisoner with very few rights, that there were many others who were hostile and unprofessional. My first experience of this was when I was asked to re-sign the police seal, on my own evidence, the evidence of my version of events. Signing the seal whilst under police interview is a procedure followed to avoid corrupt practices. Coming in with another seal to sign opened the possibility that the police had the power to break the seal and tamper with evidence.

The drive from Bridlington to Durham was long, filled with dread, as the place I was going to, HMP Low Newton, was completely unknown to me.

I could hear the staff on the van prepare their paperwork and communicate with people on the phone. Suddenly, we were there. I looked at the barbed wire outside the prison and fear coiled round my heart. I felt completely helpless, knowing that once I entered this place, there was no end in sight – no possibility of leaving – I could be here for the rest of my life. The van stopped. People were communicating by radio and some gates started to slide open. We drove into the grounds and the van stopped outside a door with bars. I was at reception.

As I sat in reception, the drivers spoke to the officers.

"She is very ill and upset."

"Let's get her in, then," one of them answered, cheerfully. I was taken into another room while they *processed* me, completed my paperwork and officially handed me over. I looked around the room, feeling completely disconnected. There was a poster on the wall, warning: *Do not give any of your personal details, such as your address, to another prisoner.* The door opened abruptly.

"Come on, then," said a dark haired, friendly woman who appeared in the doorway. I was momentarily thrown. Why was she so friendly?

"Cup of tea?" she asked, as I sat down in the processing room. "Can I have coffee?" I asked politely. I had never drunk tea in my life. She smiled a strange smile, not hostile but with the clear implication that I did not understand the language and culture in this community.

"Get her a coffee," she said to a woman wearing green trousers. I later learnt that coffee wasn't something that was regularly given to prisoners.

My coffee arrived in a blue plastic cup.

"You're not in the police cells now. Some women can't wait until they get here," she said, knowingly. Here, the staff were not glaring at me vindictively. My presence here was more irrelevant than to the police and I would come to feel like just another product in a factory-like holding centre.

"You are going onto the hospital wing," the officer stated. I didn't know what that meant. It was a wing run not by officers, but by nurses, she explained. The wing was mainly for vulnerable prisoners. For me, she explained, it was because of the trauma I was experiencing, of being charged with a serious offence. The cultures here and in the police cells were different. The staff addressed me in a more relaxed way and I was left to cope with my intense emotions. Sleeping was not an option. No matter how tired I was, I couldn't close my eyes. Every time I did close them, I could see fire.

The night officer popped his head through the bars regularly.

"OK, Michelle?" he asked, throughout the night. This was definitely a different environment to the police station.

"I didn't do it," I cried to anyone who would listen.

"Tell your solicitor," the night officer advised. "The truth will come out."

Over the next few days, being on the hospital wing taught me something about women in prison; one young lady had cut her arms so badly that the sound of the alarm bell pressed by the nurses would send several officers to help take away the sharp instrument. Prisoners made instruments and tools out of plastic knives, which we ate with, with lids of pens, in fact, just about anything you could make into a sharp edge. The same woman who had cut her arms later told me that she had been to court. She told me she had the same solicitor as me.

"Oh," I said, pleased that I had a common factor in a strange environment. She looked at me darkly, as if to warn me.

She told me, "He said you're going to get what is coming to you." How strange, I thought, for a solicitor to speak like that to another client.

The duty solicitor, independent from the police, was not looking so independent any more. The prison officers told me the difference between them and the police is that prison officers have nothing to do with the prosecution. They often hold an impartial view when holding the women and this seemed to be enough to create a totally different attitude and environment. Some of the staff in Low Newton not only held the women, but appeared to be supporting them as best as they could, in an environment which was limited to meet their needs. This new world gave me an insight into the crown prosecution service through the eyes of the prisoner I now was.

Different prisons however have different cultures, my peers told me, *and as far as prisons go, this one is ok.*

When I received evidence collected against me by the police, I was horrified. So much was exaggerated, or taken out of context.

"When we tried to tell the police information to help you, they refused to record it," some of my friends complained. One friend's mum told me the police who were collecting the information, said. *"We have been told to focus on Michelle and not Scott,"* when she told them that he had tried to run someone over the week before the murder. I would have never seen this side, had I remained free, and now I gained a new insight into how it felt to have no rights – no voice – I was unable to speak out about unfair practices. I was, after all, a woman accused of murder. It seemed hopeless. It was too late to speak out about the way the police collected their evidence, making it fit around their version, even as the witnesses complained.

The prosecution's version was one that protected both Scott and Jane and in comparison, portrayed me as the more evil.

Keith Nicholson was known to have been a long-term abuser of alcohol and other drugs. His son, Neil, had acquired the same habits and it is clear that the female defendant resented her father's adverse influence on her brother. After a period in hospital, it is clear that the female defendant became increasingly hostile to her father, which may have provided for what she and her co-accused did. She spoke to the witness Jane, about 'having to do something about her father' and asking if she knew anyone 'to give him a good kicking.'

The male defendant was arrested at 11 am on Sunday 19th September 1993 and interviewed. He gave an account of the matter wherein his co-accused had asked him, on the moors, to assault the deceased. He had refused, panicked and run away, only to be collected later in the car by the female defendant who told him that she had assaulted her father herself.

I went on to read the pile of *unused* papers, which was much bigger than the pile of prosecution papers. In that, I read about Scott's long history of abuse and beatings from his own father. I was sure that the police would start looking more to his past and realise that he was an irrational man. I wasn't to realise, then, that the prosecution would continue their investigation to be shaped around their own assumptions. Evidence would be forced in the direction of portraying Scott as the vulnerable man and not the aggressor. The missing part of the story was the instigator, Jane. I was to fit that role, too, along with being labelled a *manipulator* of Scott. Surely, they would change this view after they had spoken to more witnesses, I thought to myself.

It certainly wasn't what the prosecution psychologist had said about me. He said *I* was vulnerable.

A psychiatrist called me to an office one day. I wasn't exactly sure who he was or why he was there, I only thought someone had sent him to help me. Dr Brown wanted to ask me a few questions.

"Are you going to help me?" I asked.

"Yes, in a way, to help you," he answered.

I immediately started to offload about the unbearable flashbacks. "I can't blink without seeing them."

I felt relieved when I looked at him. I didn't really understand whether he was part of the prison system or part of the criminal justice system – it wasn't really explained – the prison seemed a separate organisation from the courts – the prosecution service was led by the police.

"How many sentences can you read in book before thinking about the incident?" he asked, studying my face closely. I thought he was trying to get me on side, gain my trust.

"I cannot read two sentences without forgetting what I have read. Are you going to help me?" I asked again.

"I am, but I need to write a report for court," he replied, "and then we can look at what help you need."

Depressingly, this turned out to be a lie. He was there to write a court report for and on behalf of the prosecution, to say that I was fit for plea and trial. He was there to gain evidence, which could be used against a defence team, which he did. My state of mind was something that the defence team would depend upon to explain my lack of assertion and action, on being taken to the middle of nowhere and not reporting the incident to the police straight away. Dr Brown's reports, based on our set of six hourly interviews, would later be used to persuade the jury otherwise.

Money and power were weighted on the side of the prosecution service and it looked as though the defence were in a boxing match with a giant. The fight was unfairly skewed from the very start and it is the start which was so very important. I had no option but to change my legal team – I had lost trust that they believed in my innocence. It seemed the psychiatrist had to get all the information he needed in a very short space of time.

'Do not speak to anyone without speaking to us first,' my new solicitor advised. It didn't matter, the psychiatrist didn't return.

The crown prosecution service, those working on the behalf of the crown, whose objective was to gain a conviction, had many guises and hats it seemed. Although he was dishonest about his visits and later used information he gained to discredit me, one line of the psychiatrist's assessment concluded that I presented signs of a vulnerable personality. This surely went in opposition to the police version of me being manipulative and controlling, although little attention was placed on his definition of me in court. If his assessment of me at that time was that I was vulnerable, then this was, perhaps, even more reason to inform me and make sure I understood who he was and why he was there. *I will stand up in court against you, on the side of the prosecution, to ensure a conviction, using anything you tell me.* So when I had asked if he was there to help me, the honest answer would have been to say, no. Then, maybe, I could have had a voice in my trial.

Being vulnerable at that time was something I couldn't understand, or see as clearly, as the whole prison could see. If they could see it, why couldn't the police? Or perhaps they could; they must have known I would comply with their request to re-sign a police tape in front of my *defence* solicitor. If they could not understand me as vulnerable, they had certainly used my vulnerable, powerless position to avoid ensuring my rights were upheld. I had a right to a fair interview. A right not to have my tapes unsealed and re sealed again out of my presence. But it had happened, and there had been nothing I could do about it.

I would see the other women from the mainstream prison, when they would come for their medication and walked through the hospital.

'Are you OK, Michelle?' women would ask, as they passed my door. It seemed they cared about my well being, even though I didn't know them. I was soon to learn there was a uniqueness in this era and in this prison, in that the women all looked after each other like family, but at the same time, they all looked lost in some way.

The Senior Officer, kept me on the hospital wing for over three months.

During that time, I received a call from my daughter, who was upset. "Nana's saying terrible things about you," she told me. My mother denied it, sending me a letter a few days later saying that my daughter was making things up, so she, my mother, had got a police officer to have a word with her. I was beside myself. My little girl was just six years old, her mother had just been snatched out of her life by police officers and now she was having to listen to her own grandmother telling her dreadful things about her mother. What had my mother been thinking about, getting a police officer involved? The extent of my helplessness engulfed me. There was nothing I could do to protect my daughter.

A few weeks later, my mother brought my daughter to visit. As they got up to leave, my daughter said she needed to use the toilet. Grasping the opportunity, I took her hand and announced, "I'm just taking my daughter to the toilet," before anyone could stop me. In the cubicle, just the two of us, my daughter's sad eyes met mine. "Mummy," she whispered, seriously, "Nana is saying *terrible* things about you."

"I know she is." I hugged my little girl, my heart breaking because I could do so little to help her. "She always has. Promise me you won't listen."

The Senior Officer called me to his office one day.

"I don't want to keep you on the hospital wing forever, Michelle, I'm moving you to the mainstream prison."

He had handpicked a middle-aged woman, Helen, who didn't really fit into the prison system, for me to share a room with. She was a motherly figure to all and even though she didn't fit in, most people liked her. They had given me a surrogate mother to look after me, my vulnerability apparent even without words.

I was given a job on the servery, serving food to the other women and taking out teas and coffees to the visitors in the visiting room. I handed out huge portions of food. If there was food left in the tins and they still looked hungry, I gave them more, instead of sending it back to the kitchen, where it would be thrown away.

There was a certain type of camaraderie in this prison. I was able to get my dress ironed for court by the laundry lady. If someone wanted something out of their property box (a box held in reception which stored things not allowed in the prison, like make up), they told the reception orderly, who would kindly take whatever you wanted out of the box and return it to the person concerned.

One day, I wasn't feeling well for work.

"It's OK," Helen told me. "You just see the doctor and you will be able to have the day off, so you can get better." As I stayed in the room during lock in, the officer game in to check bars and bells, which was something they did every day.

"Just step outside," she said, as she did to everyone following her procedure. I stepped outside my room. My cell card had been turned around and to my dismay; on the outside, I saw the letters RIP. I was terrified – I was not safe from Scott after all – he must have a helper in this prison. I looked at the officer, a hysterical laugh echoing from inside me. I went back into my cell, but my safe environment had gone. Helen returned.

"What's the matter," she said. I couldn't believe she hadn't seen the card for herself. I thought she was going along with a plot against me. They were all playing tricks on me. He was going to kill me.

Helen wouldn't let it go.

"What is wrong?"

I told her. She looked at me, relieved.

"It doesn't say RIP, it says RIC."

"What?" I said.

"Rest in Cell!" She looked concerned.

"She really is afraid for her life," I heard her tell one of the officers outside.

Another time, I got a strange letter from the prison where Scott was being held. I read it to Helen, in shock, it was obviously from a sex offender. Scott had passed on my details because he was being held in segregation.

Another inmate later came forward to my solicitor to say that Scott had bragged in prison about setting me up for a life sentence.

Spending ten months in HMP Low Newton brought a whole array of new experiences and also genuine friends; even hope that my legal team would bring justice, when I was finally bailed to a hostel in Sheffield. The probation bail team in prison pushed for it, with the support of my new legal team. And from then, I was able to experience four months of hostel life in Sheffield, being occasionally able to travel to see my daughter. In that time, I assured her I would be given a fair trial and told her, in language that a seven-year-old could understand, how a court works.

"They will tell when people are lying," I assured her. "They are there to bring justice," I told my mother. "The truth always comes out in court. It's a fair system."

Even though it seemed that the balance seemed unfair in the run up to trial, it was going to be fair in the court, I was absolutely certain of that.

Chapter 18

It was surreal, leaving the bail hostel on the morning of Monday 5th December 1994, for the start of the trial. It was a year and three months since the murder of my father.

My faithful new friend, John, sat in the taxi next to me, supporting me on that day. I had met him in the hostel in Sheffield. I needed the closeness of a friend and was drawn to John for a number of reasons. Firstly, I could be friendly with him and he wanted nothing in return. By being friendly, I wasn't seen to be or accused of flirting with him; he was gay. He was also one of the biggest drug users in Sheffield at that time, although he controlled it in such a way that it didn't affect his everyday living. In his free time, he would support me, helping me prepare for my trial.

I didn't try to explain my lack of support to him. My links with the community remained only with those friends that I had made for myself; the friends I had grown up with at school and later went on to develop at college. The most supportive person in my family was no longer here. My father. It seemed that isolation and limited networks pulled me further into the criminal justice's dark tunnel, where I remained powerless, having no one on the outside of that vast system fighting for me. I felt very much alone on the day that had not come soon enough and was not prepared, both mentally and technically, for the court's ability to morph and change its goal posts. I was glad I at least had John.

I was pleased to see my legal team when I walked through the court doors and introduced John to them. My legal team consisted of a Queens Counsel, and a female barrister by the name of Tanoo. A solicitor named Ken had come along more recently with a student solicitor called Josh. I had had several meetings with them beforehand, in order to help them to prepare for the trial. It was they who had applied for, and secured, my bail release to Sheffield.

The first time I met my QC was at Tooks Court in London. He asked me questions about what was going through my mind at the time of the offence.

He was an honest man, I could tell. He was a man I knew was fair and wanted true justice in our courts. He was an expert. What's more, he believed me.

"There is no mens rea in this case," I heard him say quietly to my solicitor, advising him of his next steps. Later, I asked what that meant: To be guilty of a crime there are two elements that have to be present. The first element is the mens rea part of the crime; the accused person has to have an *intention* to commit a crime. The other is the Actus Reus part, the action part. The QC believed, after he had questioned me, that I had no intention to commit a crime and my involvement had been frozen, almost – and he had the difficult job of explaining this to a jury.

My defence relied upon trying to explaining why I, as a gentle woman, did very little to stop the attack from happening.

Scott was brought up from the cells below to stand near me. Just the position of us seated together represented the symbol of the prosecution's case; we were standing together as co-defendants – equals, having committed a crime in partnership. The image of me being in a dock under the criminal justice system, sitting next to the man who had done the crime, surrounded by guards, portrayed a subliminal image to the jury.

Guilty until proven otherwise.

The power imbalance between defendant and the crown was never obvious to the jury, the public, or the media.

The trial was summarised for the judge as a cut-throat defence; one where both defendants were blaming each other. It crossed my mind that this could be perceived as both of us being dishonest. The prosecution focused on me, alone, to illustrate their version of events. There was a huge chunk missing in this entire story. Scott; his mind, his behaviour and *his* motive. Things that were never questioned. I remained confident that the truth would come out. I was going to have to learn how to fight now, albeit that I was trusting my barristers to do that fight for me.

A guard was seated in the middle, between Scott and me. I couldn't bear to look at him. The only two people who knew I was innocent in that court were he and I. His barrister argued that I should not be allowed to bring up his declaration to me about his daughter, "*coming on to him*", even though it would have shown that his mind was irrational and gave me a reason to really feel uncomfortable with him.

"It will turn the jury against him," they insisted.

The judge agreed. Part of my defence had been disallowed, yet I had to explain the odd relationship, without that evidence, to get them to understand that it was no joint crime.

The jury was sworn in.

"This is a cut-throat defence," the judge told the jury. It was already feeling like a nightmare.

My mother was the first on the stand. Although her police statement stated that I didn't like my father, in court, under cross-examination she changed her version. She explained that her court version was different because she felt that the police didn't, and wouldn't, let her say anything positive for me.

After my mother gave evidence, police who were acting as victim support took her home. When I called my mother that evening, she told me that they were no longer going to give her a lift to the trial. She explained also that they had not spoken to her at all in the car on the way home and she had felt very uncomfortable in their presence. It seemed that the victim's support was conditional upon a submission of evidence in the version that they had favoured. My mother was left feeling used by them. She was unable to attend the rest of the trial. The lifts stopped.

My mother also confessed on the phone that the police had said all sorts about me, but she was afraid to tell the court because she had to live in Bridlington and was afraid of the consequences.

My brother was the next on the stand. He looked vulnerable, for the first time in his life.

My brother confirmed that I was closer to my father than I was to him. He described how he found me irritating as a sister. He told the jury how he had been sitting in the car when Scott had suddenly threatened my friend Shaun with a wrench. Scott had then driven a car at Shaun, almost hitting him. Shaun had only just escaped.

My brother said he couldn't remember much of the day of the murder, due to how much he had drunk. He described how Scott had moved himself in with me and how unusually withdrawn I was after he did. He said that I always cared for my father, right up until the point that my father had been killed.

My father's best friend, Mickey, gave evidence next. He described how extremely upset he had been by the death of my father.

"Michelle loved her father," he boldly declared, "she had had a good relationship with him and clearly loved and cared for him right up to when he died." He went on to explain that the relationship wasn't as close with Neil and myself as it was with my father. He went on to say that he had warned me about Jane very early on. He described her in court as a bit of a tart and a thief who was into drugs, including amphetamines.

"She's not reliable," he told the court. "I wouldn't trust her to babysit for my children and I wouldn't believe a word she said to me."

He described my relationships, "When Michelle's relationships have broken down in the past, she always returned to her father. Men have left her. I have used her and left her as a girlfriend myself," he told the court, honestly, demonstrating my vulnerability in relationships. "She also went out with someone I knew, who treated her badly. I stopped speaking to him over it."

Mickey was asked why his evidence was different to the evidence he had given to the police. He replied that the police had misinterpreted what he said.

When Jane walked into the court, my hopes that she would tell the truth were lost in her arrogant entrance. The prosecution relied mostly on the evidence of Jane. One thing that stood out to me was that she spoke about me almost like I was not there, like I was irrelevant. Her very demeanour contradicted her version of the friend she was portraying that she had been.

She told the court that she had known me four or five years. She described to the court the illness of my brother, his blood clot on the brain. She said that I was always annoyed with my father because of it. I didn't like what he was doing, she claimed, and I wanted to sort him out so that he would stop influencing my brother's drug use. She told the jury that I wanted to teach my father a lesson and the lesson would be a good hiding, a good kicking and that I had asked her if there was anyone who could do that. She claimed she had said no. She told the court that I had broken my father's window, helping myself to a half brick out of her back garden on the day of the murder. She added that I had reported to a passing officer that there were syringes in the garden.

Later, on the way to school, she told the court, I had wanted to buy my father a bottle of whiskey to apologise for breaking the window.

"Michelle was going to do tea for them," she said, meaning my father and Neil. She didn't know whether my mother had been invited, but no one turned up. *This comment actually corroborated my evidence to the police, stating how I was trying to get them to safety.* I sat, listening in disbelief, as she altered the meanings, intentions and details of just about every aspect of what had happened that day.

Jane distanced herself from the discussions between her and Scott on the actual day of the murder. The second time she said she saw Scott that day he left a bag in her hallway, she claimed. It was a thick type carrier bag with something soft in it. He took it with him when he left, but didn't say what was in it. He asked Jane for a spade and she offered him hers. He told her he needed a new one. He also asked her for a pickaxe handle but she told him she didn't have one. She went on to say that *Michelle didn't say anything significant on the day.* The main prosecution witness told the entire court that I said nothing significant about a murder on that day.

After the day of the murder, on the Friday, she told the jury how she had come to visit me in my home, where I had confessed to hitting my father. She said it was a confession but nothing was making any sense to her. Scott hadn't said anything to her at all. She went on to say that I had confessed to her that Scott and myself had him "sorted out" and had "given him a good kicking." Although she said that she was slightly drunk (she, repeated the word 'slightly') she was sure that she was hearing a confession.

According to Jane, she just went home afterwards. On the Tuesday, four days later, she said Scott was at her house, saying bad things about me.

My barrister cross-examined Jane. She agreed with him that I had cared for my brother and my father and that reaction to being worried about my brother was a normal and healthy reaction. She agreed that Lewis was not a good influence. She agreed that I threw a brick through my father's window and that she had told me where to find one, although she continued to claim that she didn't encourage me to do it. She admitted to knowing that Scott was buying tools and putting them in the boot of the car, along with petrol. In all this time, even knowing all this information, she denied that she was part of conversation between Scott and her regarding my father. The bottle of whiskey, she agreed, was a genuine apology for upsetting my father. She said she had heard mention about some clothes being buried at Woldgate.

Jane was questioned about her honesty. She told the court she had been to court for a variety of offences. Theft and making a false statement were some of them. She was questioned about her reliability, however, she answered that she told the truth. She denied that she was blaming me to avoid being implicated in a plot with Scott. She denied that her silence over the next few days was because she had been involved.

She was also questioned about maps that were removed from

her house by the police. She said in her witness statement to the police that she had handed a map to Scott, but that she didn't know why he had wanted it. If she had provided maps, it might have suggested she was a part of the plot, by handing them over, she was covertly suggesting a place to murder my father. I had accused her, both in statements and in court, of having weapons at her house, to illustrate that she had aggressive tendencies – in court, she denied this. She did, however, admit to having her mother's air rifle. Jane denied deflecting attention away from herself, by putting it on me. She denied instigating Scott and saying it was exciting. She denied hearing Scott saying that he killed someone before, or being responsible for trying to stop me from telling anyone. She said I cared for my father but hated his involvement with drugs. In fact, she denied everything and put all of the blame onto me.

The Queens Counsel turned to the jury and questioned her reliability. He challenged her in front of the jury of having more knowledge of the plotting than I had known. She was able to give more about the detail. At that point, the jury turned to look at me, some shaking their heads in empathy. It was clear, at that point, they believed that I was not guilty, or, at the very least, they were starting to question the prosecution's case.

Mark took the stand following Jane's evidence. He told the jury that he had known Scott for a short time and had known of me for years. He told them that I had met Scott at his (Mark's) bungalow when I was with Jane. He described on the Monday night that I was screaming, asking him for help.

Mark had put himself in the best light possible, suggesting he was encouraging me to go to the police instead of preventing me. He was the last prosecution witness in the case.

At this point of the trial, it is the co-defendant's prosecution witnesses that are called. Scott's first prosecution witness was his wife. She told the court about how they separated on the 9th July. Exactly eight weeks later, he had killed my father. She said that she had no idea where he had gone to, until he told her that he was living with someone called Michelle. She described him as "wanting the best of both worlds" and he visited her often.

She repeated a version of events that he had given to her when he turned up at her house. On the Tuesday following the murder, he had gone to visit her and asked to go back to her. This is what he told her:

Michelle didn't like her father and wanted him to stop supplying her brother with drugs. She didn't get on with her Dad, but she was close to her brother. Michelle asked Scott to drive her somewhere, so he did. She had given him directions and she and Scott had gone to the moor. Michelle then asked her Dad to get out of the car while Scott remained in the car. When he got out, Michelle handed him something and told him to hit her father. Then he started to panic and he asked Michelle what was going on. He then told her he was going back to his family and ran. He didn't know how long he had been running for, but after a while, Michelle pulled up in the car and told him to get in. When she got back to the house, Michelle was calm, acting like nothing had happened.

After telling his wife this story, he stayed over that night with her and the following day, she called the police to tell them he was there.

She told the court she had seen him a couple of times and he appeared normal; on September the 12th and 14th, three to five days after the murder. It wasn't until the 19th, when he knew the police were after him, that he changed the number plates on his car and became 'upset and hysterical'. He then told her that he thought the mafia was after him. It mattered not what evidence she gave against me; I had never met her and this evidence should have been classed as hearsay.

After she finished giving her evidence and we were waiting for the next witness, it became apparent that there was something going on. An adjournment was called and it was revealed that Scott was going to plead guilty. I took a huge breath of relief – it was finally over – he was admitting his guilt! He was being honest, at last. I turned, relieved, to my barrister – the look on his face immobilised me. Something was very wrong.

It was, my legal team explained, a tactical decision by the Crown, to enable Scott to become a prosecution witness against me. He had taken a deal to have a lesser sentence, his trial ordeal over – now he was to be a witness against me. It was argued by my defence that the mere timing of this development, alone, was designed to cause maximum damage to my defence. My barrister argued that the jury should be discharged, based on this deliberate tactic.

The confession and its timing had opened a can of worms. Had he manipulated the judicial process to inflict the maximum damage on his co accused, in order to put himself in the best possible light in the regards of Tariff, (the minimum years he would serve in custody)? Had the deal depended on that timing?

My barrister argued that this trial should not continue because of the damage already done to my defence. He argued that, by allowing a joint trial, significant questioning had been allowed which would not have been allowed in a sole trial. Witnesses would not have been able to be questioned in the way that Scott's defence barrister had questioned them.

There were a number of tactics allowed in a cut-throat case, such as this had been so far, which would never have been allowed in the trial of a single defendant.

The trial, it was decided, would not continue because he was to plead guilty. The jury were taken out whilst the legal debate took place and were called back once it finished.

The jury were told the trial was stopping. They looked over to me and smiled. I believed that they thought I was going home. They were not to understand I would be facing a new trial; they had not heard the legal argument behind the scenes. Although the defence barristers agreed that a new trial should take place, the new trial would remove all of the witnesses who had said positive things about me.

The next trial was scheduled for three weeks later. It was a trial where I would stand on my own for murder. Not a cut-throat defence any longer. I was remanded into custody because of the change in my circumstances and would return to court just after Christmas. I was emotionally crushed – I had been so close to success in this trial.

Three weeks, later when I would return for another trial, I was losing hope and had very little strength. With Scott as the main witness against me, what chance did I stand?

In the three-week period between the two trials, the Christmas period of 1994, Ken, my solicitor, was asked to visit Bridlington again in an attempt to obtain any witness statements that might prove helpful in preparing for the upcoming trial. Perhaps, after the first trial, they actually realised that something else was at the bottom of this story. Everything I had said previously had come to light in the first trial.

One particular man had contacted my solicitor personally. He had shared a prison cell with Scott during that three-week period. This man informed my solicitor that he had met Scott in prison and highlighted a rumour in the prison that he was fitting me up. I don't know where those rumours came from.

The man offered a disturbing account. According to him, Scott had set his cell on fire whilst he was in it; there were several witnesses. He was known to set the prison library books on fire; he had also set a man's towel on fire whilst he was in the bath "for a laugh," according to this man. Scott, he said, had a clear problem with fire. Scott's first crime (even though he was too young to be charged with it) was setting that car on fire when he was a small boy. If what this man said was true, there was a history linking Scott and fire.

Another man came forward from Bridlington and informed the solicitor that a friend of his had told him he was at Jane's house before the actual murder and heard Scott and Jane plotting against my father whilst he was there. He thought it was a joke at the time, so he had ignored it. This version had the potential to prove what I had been saying all along – that they had discussed the plot before that day and that all they had needed was someone to blame.

There were others who had spoken at length to my solicitor, but did not want to write a statement. Others said they were afraid to stand in court, but confirmed they knew things that could potentially help me. To this date, some confirm they still do, but are too afraid, even after all this time, to write and sign a statement.

My mother had also written to the solicitors, with things she had remembered at the time of the first trial, or immediately following it. It wasn't brought to my attention at the time by my legal team, but it has been passed down to me in the pile of legal papers. In the letter to the solicitor, she recalled that Scott had confided in her, personally, that Neil would be better off without his Dad. One day, Neil and my Dad were in her house talking and Scott had sneaked in her back garden, glaring at my father through her window. The look had made my father obviously nervous and he left quickly.

It was important to understand that the enclosure of my mum's garden makes this scene even worse. No one was able to go into her back garden, except through the house, as there was, at the time, a huge building at the back of the house. The only access was through a six foot, bolted gate, which was permanently locked. The neighbour had stuck nails into the top of that gate to prevent cats going into his beloved garden. The only way in would have been to climb the fence. Why would he have done this, when the obvious way into the house was to knock on the door, as he had done so many times before? He was clearly spying on them and invading their privacy, much like he had mine. It seemed that not only was he scaring me, but my also father, at the same time. In fact, he seemed to hate us both and what's more, he was confiding in my mother.

None of these witnesses, not even my mother, were called or used at the second trial, by either the defence or the prosecution.

I didn't have sight of this letter until twenty years later, when I received all the papers from my previous solicitors.

Appearing now, only three weeks later, for yet another murder trial, knowing that there were witnesses that could help, but were reluctant to do so because they were afraid of the implications of getting involved, made me realise that, perhaps, the whole truth would not come out. I was losing hope and fast. There was also very little or no support in gaining a proper understanding or explanation of the implications the first trial would have on the second. In layman's terms, general common sense told me that the prosecution had had a rehearsal, if you like, to gain a conviction. Perhaps the defence team's hands were tied as much as mine. To fight against the prosecution was a hard thing to do. The power dynamics in court were already weighted against me.

The prosecution gave the familiar argument after the new jury had been sworn in. The majority of the press left after that version, but occasionally, one of the press members would stay to hear the defence's argument. This meant that the majority of the media were exposed to only one version of events, the prosecution version. The manipulative woman version. It seemed a recurring theme not to be given a voice at any level, once accused of a crime.

Several prosecution witnesses from the first trial, who gave evidence in my favour, were dropped by the prosecution second time around. That legal debate took place without the jury present.

I asked the defence team, "Where are some of the witnesses?"

I had no idea if they were being called or not, or if I could call them myself. I wasn't consulted and didn't know or understand the legal arguments. I trusted them blindly, in an extremely complex arena, about which I knew nothing.

The prosecution's opening argument changed slightly this time. They added this time that I had cared for my father, but he preferred the company of his drug using friends. It seemed the line of argument of dislike for my father had disappeared along with the first trial. If the jury was to hear that I liked my father in this trial and it wasn't proved, perhaps they would lose their case?

Scott, rather than Jane, was now the main prosecution witness and he took the stand against me as the first witness. He had given a new statement to the police between the two trials. This was now his 5th version of what happened and he fully disclosed to the jury, through the questioning of the Queens Counsel, that he was giving this new evidence as part of a deal to secure a lesser tariff.

The Queens Counsel read out all of his previous versions asking him to clarify the correct version. He declared it was his fifth version, the one that would provide him a reduction in his sentence.

The QC questioned his lack of remorse, reminding him that he went to see his wife on the day of the murder to organise his maintenance payments. He suggested this to illustrate that Scott's attitude was cool, calm and calculated.

Version five had painted a calculating picture, or rather the prosecution did. The police had always taken the stance that he was of lower rate intelligence, easily manipulated. His new statement fitted the crown version more closely than any of his previous versions.

Jane's second time in court, she looked guarded and not as confident or as arrogant as she had done in the first trial. She appeared more careful and worried. She had been exposed in the first trial.

She gave some small background to her experience of my family, stating she had known us about four years. She said we were a close family and despite problems, we all cared for each other. I had cared about my family, but wanted them to stop taking drugs. She told the court that my mum and I had really blamed my father for the blood clot on my brother's brain, although I stood by both my Dad and Neil. She had never before seen anything remotely like the behaviour I now stood accused of. I was a quiet, mild mannered person. On 9th September she saw a natural reaction and 'spontaneous explosion' of anger and that I had genuinely apologised to my father.

Scott, she said, didn't go to work and was looking after Neil, taking his health more seriously.

Jane now changed her account of the conversation between her and Scott in her kitchen, giving the same version as I had given to the police sixteen months ago. She was starting to say *exactly* the same things that I had.

So far, the murderer had given evidence, Jane was now openly admitting her discussions with him; Jane's cousin, whom I didn't really know and Jane's brother in law and ex-boyfriend were still to take the stand.

Lewis was next. My father's friend, who wasn't his friend. He was subpoenaed, meaning that he was forced to attend. All the comments he made were negative. It was obvious he didn't like me. He described himself as being 'wrecked' on the day of the murder. What the jury didn't hear was that he had turned up at my mother's house a few days after my father's disappearance. My father owed him money, he claimed, and if he wasn't paid, he'd be back to break the windows.

Mark came to the dock. The only negative comment he made was about the whiskey being involved. He was correct in a way. Yes, the bottle of whiskey was used in the car by Scott, therefore, it was involved. Although a bottle of wine bought by him previously and drugs also brought by him were being used, the bottle of whiskey was bought by me earlier in the day. I had told Mark that my father had been plied with whiskey in the car. Somehow, he came to the conclusion that if the whiskey was involved, then I must have been, too.

Under cross examination by the Queens Counsel, Mark asked him to explain the meaning of a word in his statement. The Queens Counsel asked him why he needed his statement explaining, asking, "It's your statement ... or is it?" The judge immediately shot the defence team down, before Mark could answer.

This hint of police interference was starting to leak out in several areas. One in interview with me, when they had told me, "Mark does not believe you, now we have finished with him."

And he didn't, it was clear.

It reminded me of an accusation I had made that information in my recorded interviews on police tapes was missing. *Where had it gone?* The judged had prevented *that* witness from answering as well. The police were not on trial, he insisted, I was. The judge's role is to ensure a fair trial. If the police were not on trial, however, surely if something comes up in that trial to suggest an unfair or corrupt practice, isn't it the judge's place to make that information transparent, or even to look into it?

In the case of Mark's statement, perhaps a discussion, at that point, with the witness, about the context of how his statement was taken, asking him if his statement was taken in a fair and professional way, would have been enough? Nobody should be immune from being questioned about corrupt practices in court, not least those professionals who work in or for it.

Mickey's girlfriend's statement was read out.

'Michelle contacted me by phone. She spoke fast. She said she needed to speak to Mickey, to get help.'

No one contested that statement, just as in the first trial.

The main question for the jury was obvious to me. Why, if someone is innocent, would it take six days to go to the police? It does make a person look guilty, even I could see that.

Chapter 19

The end of the trial was near and my anxiety and stress was reaching its peak. Despite all that was said, I was sure the real evidence would clear my name. After the prosecution gave their speech, mainly about me being manipulative, the Queens Counsel stood up to give his final speech to the jury. He told them.

This is a terrible case; however you look at it. The wasted lives involved in it hardly bear thinking about. And again, DRUGS have devastated yet another family with lasting effects, which will be felt for decades to come. Keith Nicholson is dead, murdered up on the North York Moors. Many years before that happened, Carol and he split up. Neil nearly died from a blood clot in his brain and has clearly wasted much, if not all, of his younger years. Even after that devastating illness, it would appear that Keith Nicholson and Lewis continued to supply him with drugs, which they encouraged him to take. Michelle Nicholson stands charged with the murder of her father. A young woman, in reality, of good character, non-violent, according to other witnesses, and who appears to have come from a close family who really care for each other, and for whom the only real stain was drugs. Even her daughter will not be immune to these events. The tragedy of the last year will have left its effect on her, probably forever.

NOW WHAT DID THE FAMILY DO ABOUT THOSE DRUGS?

It is clear that they coped with them and had done so, as best they could, for years. They never gave up on each other. They argued; they tried to arrange counselling and persuasion was brought to bear on the men to stop, but there were visits, and presents, and support. Even after the dreadful illness of Neil, even after he went back to live with his father and went back onto drugs, Michelle and her mother did not turn their backs on Keith Nicholson. Two witnesses agreed that, without hesitation. The pattern that emerged is that Michelle and Denise were loyal, caring, extremely worried and they, certainly Michelle, sometimes got upset.

Now the prosecution have to say that on 8th/9th September 1993, all that changed with Michelle. That way of behaving, established over years, suddenly went and was replaced by the absolute opposite. From being an anxious and upset, but supportive, member of the family, Michelle became a cool, calculating and utterly brutal murderer. Because this was no spontaneous blow with the breadknife, but a thought out and mercilessly executed plan. You may think that such a change is totally unlikely, particularly when we bear in mind the upset way in which Michelle was behaving on the 9th. The taking back of the pictures and the guitar; getting a policeman to go and look at the syringes in the garden; the brick through the window are all consistent with natural human emotions, none of which have anything to do with murder.

THE NEW DEVELOPMENT IN THAT FAMILY WAS NOT A CHANGE BY MICHELLE, BUT THE ARRIVAL OF THE PERSON WHO WE CAN NOW SEE AS THE EXTREMELY SINISTER SCOTT

You are going to have to make a very careful assessment of him. You will no doubt arrive at conclusions as to the manner of man that he is; what makes him tick; what he is capable of; why he murdered Keith Nicholson; and whether he did that alone or not.

Indeed, the conclusions you arrive at in relation to him will probably be crucial as regards your ultimate decisions about Michelle Nicholson.

Did he manipulate or was he manipulated?

Did he carry out Michelle Nicholson's bidding, or did this strange man you saw in the witness box decide wholly for himself what he thought needed to be done and then set about executing his own plan on Keith Nicholson?

WHO WAS THE MANIPULATOR?

The prosecuter opened the prosecution's argument clearly, and over-boldly to you:

"The picture that is she, Michelle Nicholson is the manipulator (said the prosecutor) of people, information and events. As the story unfolds, you will see that emerge".

The evidence in fact, you may think, revealed nothing like it. Quite the contrary.

We suggest that they have to say something like that, in order to make their case even begin to work; that without such a suggestion, they could not even start to argue sensibly that Michelle is a father killer. And does it not also, saying that, sow the seed of prejudice in your minds against her. For they are cleverly suggesting that she is manipulating you.

WHAT IS THE EVIDENCE ON THIS ISSUE? Rather than the prosecution's (beguiling) hints and submissions.

They met at Mark's.

Who was in need of somewhere to live, that would be better than a bedsit? Who would be wanting a new life quickly, having just left a long marriage?

Scott.

So there was a mutual attraction between the two of them, yes, but the one with the real need for a quick conquest at the time was Scott. Michelle Nicholson goes to Plymouth for a short break with her mother. She asks Scott to look after things while she is away. He is asked to feed the pets, that sort of thing. You may think he simply takes advantage of her absence, and her easy going nature, and moves in, lock stock and barrel. That does not have the feel of a manipulated man to it. Quite the reverse.

He is taking control. Making decisions for himself, deciding on what he wants, and going for it, without even beginning to ask her permission. He accepts that she is angry when she gets back, and then he makes up this story about her being cross about a diary that has gone missing. The reality is, you may think, that she is upset at his taking her over. Like a cuckoo in the nest, he takes over this family in the most extraordinary way. The unfortunate and ruined Neil, he makes his friend. He does not seem to have any other life of his own, but instead tries to make himself crucial to the Nicholsons.

He gives Neil a job.

He goes to see KW, from the Alcohol Advisory Service in Hull on 2nd September with Neil and suggested to KW that he should advise Neil that it would be better for him not to live with his father, because Scott believed that Keith was pressuring Neil to abuse drink and drugs. Scott also asked if KW could arrange a detoxification programme for Neil in hospital. This is a classic example of Scott taking over the family, and organising and controlling their lives. He spends his days driving people around. He is endlessly obliging and helpful. The interesting question is whether this is because he is being manipulated, or rather because he wishes to make himself indispensable to the family. By ingratiating himself, he ensures that he will, in the end, run the show. That they find they cannot do without him.

That this is the correct interpretation is shown in his approach to this case. At every turn, what he did was an attempt to get the best deal for himself. His changing accounts were all designed to help him. He admitted that the only person he was worried about was himself, and that he gave the different versions of events in attempts to secure the best result for himself.

What does that tell you about manipulation? If you want examples of someone in this case controlling events, and trying to use people, that is it.

VERSION 1

This is delivered while breaking down in tears at his wife's home. Fearful that the mafia are after him, so he claims. Saying that he was afraid that he was going to die and that he would be unable to say anything about the mafia.

First, is not there something quite off the wall about that? Something more than a little mad? There is not a shred of evidence from anyone that Keith Nicholson had friends of that kind.

Second, he is not worried about the body that he has left wretchedly up on the moors. Instead, his only concern is that people who he cannot control may be after him. He is self-interested, unconcerned about others, and only trying to protect number one.

VERSION 2

He agreed with his wife that he will have to give himself up, even though he tried to hide with relatives and changed the number plates on his car. She, no doubt, gets him to calm down. He asks her to wash clothes for him. Showers, has a meal, and then gives his second version. It is a lie. It *involves trying to put together an account which will protect him and wholly incriminate Michelle Nicholson. There is no manipulation of Scott in that. In this account, Michelle Nicholson does all the planning. She organises the route; gets the weapons; and on the moors screams and shouts at Scott, telling him to hit Keith; he claims he sees her hit her father and he does not do so. He has the gall, in this account, to accuse Michelle of being mental and evil. (Terms which are far more apt to describe himself).*

VERSION 3

This is given to the police in interview, after he has had many days to compose himself and to decide on how best to turn affairs to his advantage. It comes after talking matters over with his wife.

And the account that is given is not from a man who is sorry for what he has done, having been made, as the Prosecution would have it, the victim of his love for a determined woman. To the contrary, he has now changed the account he worked out at home and which his wife heard. He has refined it. Improved it. Made it even more damning against Michelle, and even better for himself. He begins here by saying the he only knew that Keith had been killed up on the North Yorkshire Moors, because he had read about it in the press. In the first version he accepts he saw at least one weapon, that Michelle tried to get him to use it on her father.

Now he says that he saw no weapons or blows at all.

He simply ran off. Left her to kill her father. And was then picked up by Michelle Nicholson when she was driving away.

He claimed falsely that he went up twice afterward to try and find the body. THAT WAS A STARK LIE.

Interestingly, in this account he claimed that it was a real possibility that Michelle had planned it with Jane. (What he was turning around there, one wonders?)

193

He also keeps the Mafia angle running in this account.

He agreed, in evidence before you, that this story was a complete lie and was designed to pull the wool over the eyes of the jury, who were sworn in to decide this case in December.

He kept those lies and falsehoods going throughout the trial, and only gave up on it when he decided that it stood no chance of success.

So, not because he felt guilty about what he had done, but because he wanted to turn events, yet again, to his advantage.

His Honour and the Home Secretary have to make an assessment as to how long he will serve in prison, as a result of the life sentence he will inevitably receive.

You may remember that he literally took the sentence about "The Tariff" (as it is called) out of my mouth. He knows exactly what is involved, and again, he is trying to manipulate events for himself.

VERSION 4

This was supposed to be the truthful account, set out in his witness statement of 10th December. 1994, which was now finally being told as a result of his change of plea to Guilty, with him now being the principle prosecution witness.

No such luck.

Even then, he told untruths on his own admission, and he was seen in prison by his lawyers about this account he had given, with police officers also trying to get in to see him. He would not see the police, and on the morning of his trial he put the finishing touches to.

VERSION 5.

This changed the account over what the petrol and the shovel were for. In Version 4 he claimed that they were to burn and bury clothes. On his final account, this too is untrue. He now says that the idea was to put the body in a hole, and to burn it with petrol to hamper identification. And he hopes now that His Honour and the Home Secretary will be persuaded to deal more leniently with him than they will with Michelle Nicholson?

Not once, in all of his long account, did he express an ounce of sorrow for what he did that night, on his own admission, to a man he scarcely knew. We have heard nothing about his psychological make up. One would not be surprised to learn that the man is quite mad. And the lies, of course, continue. This piece of curtain, which was wrapped around the pick axe handle during the blows which he delivered, which he says just happened to slip off when Michelle, on his account, set about her father, was never found, notwithstanding an exhaustive search on the moors. It never existed. He made that up so that he could pretend that he had no responsibility for the serious injuries.

HIS ACCOUNT

Central to it is his claim that there was a cold and calculating plot, involving Michelle Nicholson, that Keith Nicholson will be harmed, and that this turns quickly into the decision that he will be killed. That is hatched on Wednesday 8th September in the evening, certainly in so far as the harm is concerned, and very possibly the assassination. So, according to Scott, Michelle Nicholson has that night begun laying her evil plans.

How does that fit with her known behaviour the following morning? All of it is the spontaneous, human and emotional reaction of her seeing Neil, out of his head, after Keith and/or Lewis have provided him with a very large shot of drugs, be it Morphine tablets or an injection of a cocktail of drugs. She does things, all of which were calculated to bring attention on herself.

She takes back the pictures, and throws them away.

She hides the guitar at Jane's.

She dramatically lobs a brick through the window. Coming back, according to Jane saying, "That will teach him".

And more than anything else, she involves a police officer, who sees her upset, while she even tells him what she is upset over, in general terms, namely the drug taking at her father's house. If she had really decided on a course that was to be taken, namely that Keith would be harmed or killed, none of that would have happened. She would have bided her time, waiting until the evening came round, when she could have relied, to use Lewis's expression, on her father being wrecked on drink and drugs, and that would have needed no whiskey from her.

All of that behaviour cuts across and destroys the evidence of Scott on the evening of 8th Sept, that they had agreed on the course of action, or part of it. As far as established physical acts are concerned, what does she do?

Buys a bottle of whiskey. No more.

(On that subject, I remind you in passing what, the chemist, told you – that, contrary to the Prosecution's original theory, the likely 180 alcohol level from a heavy drinker may well not result in them being that drunk. And the drugs were either in low quantities, or unquantifiable, or could be from days before, or were a neutralising mix of stimulants and suppressors)

What on the other hand does Scott do?

He spends hours that day with the man he has adopted, Neil Nicholson. He is unable to go to work because he is so upset about it all. Jane said that he was taking his condition very seriously. Lewis also said how concerned Scott was.

He turns down the offer of Jane's garden tools, but instead insists on buying new implements to kill and dispose of Keith Nicholson. And he goes out to buy just such implements.

He says in front of Jane that "he can do something about Keith Nicholson".

HOW DOES THAT FIT WITH SCOTT'S EVIDENCE THAT THIS WAS ALL PLANNED IN IMPORTANT RESPECTS THE NIGHT BEFORE?

He knows there is a full can of petrol, and says in the presence of Jane that he needed petrol.

While he is doing those things, he goes and sees his wife about the maintenance payments. While he putting the finishing touches to his plans to do away with this man, he is arguing with his wife over her weekly income. There is something truly chilling about that. He is crucially present when the route, and the road and the town names on the way to the North Yorkshire Moors are written down. He ensures that he has that for the drive. He, on his own admission, is active and deeply involved in all of that.

What does Jane say about Michelle Nicholson?

She sat watching the television. All the activity was by Scott. She was quiet, and did not seem to react when he said, "He could do something about him". She just let him get on with whatever he was doing.

Now the map book. Crucially, Jane agrees that, exactly as Michelle Nicholson told you in evidence and in her interviews, that Scott and Jane were in the kitchen together, looking at the map, and she, Michelle, was simply left sitting watching television in the living room. Jane said that Scott was looking at the map while she was getting on with her own work.

NO WONDER AFTERWARDS MICHELLE NICHOLSON THOUGHT THAT THEY HAD PLOTTED IT TOGETHER,

BOTH HAVING BEEN, ON JANE'S ACCOUNT, IN THE KITCHEN TOGETHER.

So the only other person present, the second main prosecution witness, contradicts Scott and wholly agrees with Michelle Nicholson. Throughout all the planning, Michelle was watching

Television, NOT doing any of the things Scott tried to pretend she was.

From everything she saw, Jane concluded that Michelle was making a genuine apology for the broken window when she gave the bottle of whiskey. So, for Jane, this allegedly sinister bottle was no more than a real attempt to make up for her dramatically breaking her father's living room window.

Scott claimed that on the night following the death of Keith Nicholson, Michelle was boasting about how she hit her father. Not so, according to Jane. Her recollection is markedly different.

Michelle was in some kind of trance. She was just talking. It seemed as though her behaviour was as a result of her being upset, as she had been on the Thursday. She agreed that because she (Jane) was so drunk, she may be mistaken about Michelle saying that she had hit her father. That it may have been that all the violence was done by Scott.

WHAT DOES SCOTT DO AFTERWARDS????

He coolly:

Disposes of the clothes and the implements during two trips up to Woldgate.

Cleans out the car so well, that the forensic expert says that the car was in an exceptionally clean condition, being devoid of any of the usual contents.

He leaves to stay with a relation he scarcely knows. There do not seem to be any proper friends who he can turn to for advice and sensible help as to what he should do.

Instead, he walks out with a television to sell to his father.

He ends up with a family member. She had not seen anything much of *him for 15 years. He goes to church with her and other members of the family. During what are described as "normal" conversations, he simply says that he had split up from his wife and that he has plans to go back to her.*

On 16th September, he is once again back running people around, this time taking his mother to the Halifax Infirmary. Winning people over by being obliging.

He visits his father. He is quite able to talk to him normally, and sell the television to him, giving absolutely no indication that anything was wrong, presenting as calm, and happy to be going back to his wife.

This is 7 days after he has murdered someone in horrific circumstances. His lack of emotion was borne out by what you heard of him. A family member said that he always bottled things up. All quite weird and inexplicable.

SO LET US PUT SCOTT TO ONE SIDE FOR A MOMENT-LET US LOOK AT WHAT THIS CASE REALLY COMES TO

Michelle Nicholson cares for both father and brother

Brother nearly dies.

When he goes back onto drugs, she is understandably upset.

On 9th Sept, she acts spontaneously and understandably.

The brick, pictures, guitar, and telling a policeman about the syringes in the garden....

Having seen Neil, having got really upset and remaining upset, she goes and sits in the living room at Jane's and lets Scott get on with whatever he is doing, paying no attention to his activities and planning. She organises the family for tea and tried to get Neil and Keith to join them. She buys a bottle of whiskey, which Jane thinks was a wholly genuine gift. Having made up with her father, after a very dramatic day, she spends the evening with him, trying no doubt to be a friendly daughter. Apart from Scott, the only person who suggests that Michelle was involved in Scott attempts to get Keith out of the house was Lewis. That is the only suggested evidence of planning on Michelle's part, once Jane's evidence is understood properly.

What a witness for the prosecution to rely on in a murder trial.

He has about as bad a criminal record as one could imagine. Over a hundred different criminal cases, covering almost every type of crime apart from the most serious such as this. A long term drug and alcohol abuser. He was arrested under suspicion of murder and even then had a drug user kit of syringes and potions on him. A man who, on his account, was wrecked when any conversation took place. He had a strained relationship with Michelle Nicholson. A friend of Keith, who, if he was honest, you may think would have blamed Michelle, however much the truth maybe otherwise. For you to be asked to rely on the evidence of someone like that, so that you can be sure, is quite extraordinary and appalling. You would not convict the Prince of Darkness on the evidence of this man.

AND THEN HER PRESENCE ON THE JOURNEY AND AT THE SCENE AND HER STAYING WITH SCOTT AFTERWARDS.

Is she to be convicted for that?

Is her "inactivity" alone going to turn her, in your eyes, into a father killer?

IN THE LIGHT OF WHAT YOU HAVE HEARD IN THIS COURT, THAT, WE SUBMIT TO YOU, WOULD BE A WHOLLY UNFAIR AND WRONG CONCLUSION, AND WE ASK YOU TO RECALL CAREFULLY ALL YOU HAVE HEARD IN EVIDENCE ABOUT THIS PERIOD.

This strange man comes into her life. According to one of the prosecution's main witnesses, she soon wishes him gone. Mark told you that the relationship went wrong quickly. Before Keith went missing, Scott refused to leave her home and Michelle Nicholson was stuck with him. And then, he shows his capacity for violence. From being the quiet and obliging taxi driver and everything else, he suddenly changes and follows her around. Just ~~because Michelle has been seen in the car of an old boyfriend, he then drives~~ his car at Shaun, nearly hitting him, because he has a bag of clothes in the boot of his car, and because they had a plan to go out somewhere with other friends that night. You may think that a witness gives the right account of this. If he had not jumped over the fence, Shaun would have been seriously injured, or worse you may think. And remember that odd knife in the vent of the Cortina. Hidden there. It is revealing about the man.

Now *ACUTE STRESS DISORDER*

The prosecution try to pour scorn on this.

They have to. Because this provides the proper psychological explanation for Michelle Nicholson's passivity and inactivity. That mental disorder, when taken together with the fear that she felt for Scott. With this disorder, one looks for a traumatic event which involved the threatened death or serious injury of oneself or another. Although Dr Brown would not have it, Dr Jones was sure that the new threat to Neil's life, through drugs, would have amounted to this. We should never forget that recently, he had nearly died. Then a cocktail of drugs was injected into him, and Michelle sees him after 17 Morphine Tablets had taken hold of him, and this surely would have just such an effect. Leaving her feeling intensely fearful and helpless. Once that happened, Dr Jones would expect her to be subject to a sense of numbing, detachment, and absence of emotional responsiveness. Does that not fit exactly with what Jane describes during the day of Thursday 9th September, Michelle just sitting watching the television, seemingly not engaging at all with what Scott is saying or doing. Seeming to pay it no regard at all.

Michelle Nicholson is not going to know how to fake Acute Stress Disorder. Like many people, she would not even have heard of it, let alone know what to do to make her description of what she did and felt afterwards fit that particular mental disorder.

How does she describe this in interview?

"He had taken a cocktail of drugs … the doctor had told us that if he ever took any more drugs, it could be it for him, he could go in to a coma. I was upset. I was annoyed." (page 30).

At page 36 "He was absolutely drugged".

At page 46 after Neil had tried to hit her "I was shaking and upset".

Against that background, she tells the police at page 51 that Scott said at Jane's that he "could get rid of me Dad."

And her reaction at page 52 "I didn't really know what he meant by that. I was still upset. I was not listening".

At page 52 "I was sat in the living room, watching the television. I was in a daze. I was still upset." She talks to the police about sitting quietly watching the television, and not saying anything. At page 85 she tells the police she was not involved in any discussions.

Those pages around 85 and 86 are central. Although she suspected something, in her mind it was not going to happen. "It was just not going to happen in my mind." "It was just like being in a dream. I didn't really think it was gonna happen." At page 109, she did not think that anything was going to happen to her father because she had already had a word with him about it. Page 214, "I did not think in my brain that it would happen," Page 217 "I had suspicions … I was in a daze." And then, by the time they were in the car, and on this dreadful journey, her daze like state has added to it her fear of Scott. — page 119 "I had a suspicion that something was gonna happen. I was frightened, I was upset, I didn't know what to do … I repeatedly asked Scott to turn back…" She got changed up on the

Moor because she was frightened. He was getting angry. "I was frightened," page 124. Then "I got changed because I was frightened," page 125. Over and over she tells the police that "I didn't want it to happen," page 221 and "It wasn't going to happen," page 222. Why does she stay with him in the days which followed? This could again so easily, so understandably, be both her fear, and a combination of *Acute Stress Disorder,* followed by, or having added to it, *Post-Traumatic Stress Disorder.* These well-known mental disorders being further complicated by the remarks that Scott makes about getting guns and the people who may die if he is arrested. All of that would rob a person of their usual human responses. Just as other mental disorders have the effect of making us behave differently, so these less well known, but wholly recognised, disorders have the effect of stopping us from behaving as most of us would, most of the time. Instead of running to family, friends or the police, and saying, nay screaming, "Look what he has done," she sits, like a frightened rabbit trapped in the headlights of an oncoming car, unable to react or do anything sensible. Sitting with a duvet wrapped around her, rocking backwards and forwards, just speaking to the room, reliving what had happened, to a drunk Jane, and the sinister Scott, who according to Jane was not drinking much, but just sat close by, not talking. It sends shivers down your spine, to think about his brooding presence. Of the time afterwards when she is with Jane, she says at page 189, "I was just in shock. I was sick." The following day, there is the odd description of the cup, and Scott saying there was a spider in it and the way this led her to be sick, and to "start freaking out all day, crying," as she described it at page 195/6. On one opportunity when she got away briefly from him, she went banging on doors, and people who saw her could tell she was distressed, page 208 and 209. As she says in interview at pages 204 and 205, "I did not go to the police for a week because I was upset about my Dad, I was upset for my brother and my mum. I was frightened of Scott. And what might happen to me. I believed that Scott was capable of getting a shotgun and carrying out his threats".

"I do not know where he is now. He said if I ever say anything and he gets arrested, he'll kill whoever arrests him." etc

At page 199 to 202, she had talked to the Detective Inspector about him getting nasty, and saying he could get a shot gun at any time, and that he was going to sort something out. "It was going round and round in my mind. I was cracking up."

She does not regain any sensible response until the night when, having been at Mark's house, she finally feels the courage to shout and scream and insist on being taken away from Scott, so that she can be with a friendly and caring person who she can talk to, and put herself in a frame of mind where finally she can tell this dreadful truth to the world, that she was present when her ex-boyfriend lured her father to a lonely spot, and then killed him.

And what do the prosecution do with this occasion when she tells, for the first time, the consistent account she has always given of what happened and what her role was? They simply try to turn even this against her, and to portray her as promiscuous and manipulative. In examination in chief of Mark, the prosecution used the word 'sex' 16 or 17 times when obtaining his account of their relations.

Of course, the alternative is that Mark is a safe port in a hurricane. That having watched the most terrible thing on the Moors, and no doubt feeling profound guilt because she had not stopped him, and for having not told her mother and brother, she is able to find finally some comfort from the nightmare, and basic human warmth in his arms.

Sex sex sex, rail the prosecution.

A frightened, traumatised and deeply shocked young woman would be far closer to the truth. And when thinking about that, what does she do, on Mark's account, after she has told him this terrible news. She does not stay to go to bed with him, but having been cuddled and comforted by him, she goes home to be with her daughter. Sitting in court 2 in Sheffield, it is easy to say, we would have done this or done that. It is easy to say that she should not have stayed with Scott afterwards.

And THOSE ACCOUNTS.

To: Mark – she "just came out with it" he said, and that when she was talking "she just was not herself," namely you may think that she was still suffering from mental disorder. Tears rolling down her face, with her just staring at the wall while she told him. At times, she was shaking and was very upset, according to Mark. He said that you could see that she was frightened.

Her aunt (No one suggests that a different account was given to her aunt)

WPC Marie (nothing in the way Michelle Nicholson spoke to her that made her believe that Michelle was anything other than genuine).

The police in interview

Dr Brown

Dr Jones

To you

There is no hint, from anyone, that there is any serious discrepancy in what she says. Minor matters such as when she first started thinking about things like guns, and exactly how much she realised about Scott's intent, yes, but nothing of significance. Her version of events, often delivered when she is upset and really anguished, and given over many months, never varies. And, we submit, that is not because she is some legendary actress, but because *HER CONSISTENT ACCOUNT IS WHAT HAPPENED.* Even down to the number of times her father is hit by Scott. The 9 separate injuries are found, and she says he is hit 10 or more times.

So the accounts she gives are:

Consistent between themselves, and they do not materially change as time goes by (and that should be contrasted with Scott) and consistent with her suffering from Acute Stress Disorder and later after [her father] has died, with Post Traumatic Stress Disorder.

THE LIKELY COURSE OF EVENTS IS AS FOLLOWS:

Scott leaves his wife after many years. He seems to have no other life. Moves in on Michelle Nicholson and her family

She says she wants him out (as Mark agrees) He refuses to go. He becomes very close to Neil, and keeps some sort of unbalanced obsession for Michelle. (Again Mark talks about how obsessed he was with her). One of his chief characteristics seems to be his desire to do what he thinks will make people like him. All this driving around, and being obliging. He sees Neil badly drugged up. He has attempted to keep him away from Keith, as was shown by the visits to the drugs counsellor. To win Michelle back in some crazy way? To solve a problem? To help this family in an insane fashion? He carried this out. All the tidying up and burning afterwards. He meets little real opposition from Michelle because of her fear of him and her mental disorder.

AGAINST THAT

Do you think that this young woman planned and mercilessly executed her father? On Scott's account, because of the curtaining, she would have been responsible for all the serious injuries, and including the huge blow that would have been required to cause that much considerable injury to the cheek.

That just defies belief. As does the suggestion that she suddenly went from a caring and concerned daughter into a calculating father killer. If Scott had not forced himself into this family, this would never have happened. He mercilessly killed her father, and now he is attempting, equally mercilessly, to drag her down with him, so as to improve his position on sentence, so he hopes.

Her life has been seriously damaged by this dreadful killing. We ask you not to destroy it completely by complying with Scott's wishes, and returning a verdict of guilty to murder.

A word about MANSLAUGHTER.

Quite regardless of all other issues, the effect of Neil's near death, and seeing him back on the drugs which would probably kill him, and which had been given to him by his father, fundamentally affected Michelle Nicholson's normal way of viewing the world. We submit the result of that was to give her Acute Stress Disorder, which made her unresponsive and in a daze etc. Unable to intervene in what Scott set about doing, and therefore not guilty of any offence. But the strength of the reaction was such as to mean that, for the reasons that His Honour will explain, both Provocation and Diminished Responsibility become options, which you have to consider. I am not going to address you on them now, because we submit that she is not guilty of murder or manslaughter. But given the facts of the case, of the two, manslaughter is the only sensible option. So if this ever becomes a live issue, we ask you to dismiss murder on the basis of all that you have heard, and what is probable, and to concentrate only on whether she is not guilty or guilty of manslaughter. We hope that by now you are sure of her innocence. But that is not the test. We submit that it must a million miles from that. The account she gave you and has given throughout, when considered by you and set against all the prosecution evidence, should lead, we submit, clearly and correctly to a verdict of not guilty.

Chapter 20

Following my barrister's speech, the judge gave a direction to the jury. The first half was very favourable and then it was adjourned. After coming back, it seemed to have become very weighted against me. The QC had left straight after his speech and had gone on to another trial.

The judge, in the second half of his directions to the jury, made reference to Jane's evidence. I didn't understand what he was getting at.

He said something like, 'What you need to remember is that, although Jane said she was present at the time of the plotting and not Michelle, it was Michelle that was at the murder scene at the time of the murder.' (Unfortunately the actual records have long since been destroyed, something which has made the fight to clear my name so much more difficult.)

Surely Jane had been discredited on the stand? He was using my presence at the scene, alone, to tell them they could convict me, on the basis of having knowledge that something *might* happen.

(This reasoning, I would find out many years later, was based on a legal doctrine called "Joint Enterprise." In 2016, the Supreme Court ruled that it had been being misapplied for thirty years.

The Supreme Court ruling meant that cases being tried under the Joint Enterprise doctrine needed to show the *intention of murder* by any secondary parties. In other words, just being somewhere where a murder is committed is not enough – the courts have to prove that you, as a "secondary party" *intended* that a murder be carried out.)

The jury went out. It was now a waiting game. I sat in my cell praying, hoping that they would be able to understand. Half way through that day, three of the jurors wanted information on "cumulative provocation." The barrister said that was not a good sign. My solicitor, on the other hand, was hopeful. He said it was a sign that they were struggling to convict. The judge gave information on cumulative provocation and diminished responsibility – these were defences my team had not used.

I'm sure it was not an easy job for the jury. But even today, I knew those three jurors were taking the trial the most seriously. They wanted the truth. They nodded their heads in encouragement when I was trying to hold onto the strength to speak. After two days, the jury was still undecided. The judge reminded them, quite forcefully, that their verdict had to be unanimous. The jury returned to the courtroom one hour later.

The guards seemed tense. "Has it come back yet?" I heard them talking quietly outside of the door. "No verdict yet."

"It's back!"

I felt like they were all rooting for me in unspoken empathy. Some came and told me that they believed me. I know I had a lot of support, down there waiting in the cell. The cell door opened. The female guard was expressionless. "The verdict's in."

"That's good," I said, wearily. It was over.

Standing in the dock, I watched the foreman walk through the door, leading the jury. He looked over to my mum and smiled. She smiled back. *That's a good sign*, I thought. My brother Neil, sitting beside her, looked tense.

"How do you find the defendant," the judge asked, "guilty or not guilty of murder?"

"Guilty!"

I thought I had misheard. My solicitor looked horrified.

The courtroom slowed down. Everyone in the room was looking at me. The barristers, even the prosecution barrister, looked defeated.

The police looked victorious, smiling and laughing amongst themselves.

It's a mistake ... they will say it's a mistake in a minute. I was completely unable to process the enormity of the decision they had made for my life.

"Come on," the woman beside me said, gravely. I knew she was with me. She took my hand and arm to lead me back to my cell. Back downstairs, although she was close by, I could hear only her voice from a distance.

"She is in shock ... don't close her door."

People walked past and peered in. The cell was spinning.

"You must drink something," she said, holding out a cup of water. I didn't look at her, holding on to the wall for the strength to stand up and keep my balance.

"You're going up for sentencing in the next ten minutes. Scott will be in the dock with you ... you have to be strong." She spoke with genuine empathy.

That's when I begged.

"Please, no! I can't go up in the dock and stand next to him, knowing he's won. He killed my father and now he's taking me down with him. Please ask them to sentence me without me being there."

"They can't. You have to go."

"Why," I beseeched her. "I can't do it."

I couldn't bear to stand next to my father's killer, knowing that only he and I knew the truth. I couldn't bear that people thought I could have done such a heinous crime.

"You can," she reassured me, brusquely. "I'll be there to hold your hand … I'll be right with you." I remembered how safe I had felt, walking in the street holding my father's hand, when I was a little girl.

"Come on, it's time to go." Ten minutes had already passed, it felt like ten seconds. "You can do it … hold on to my hand."

That's when I found myself walking the cold dark staircase in complete, indescribable shock. It was cold, bleak and dark and a gripping sense of horror engulfed me to the point where I thought it would take away my breath entirely. The shock was so intense, I felt as though it might even take my young life.

Looking up to the top of the stairs, I knew I had no option but to climb them.

I knew, too, that *he* would be standing next to me, victorious, knowing that he had not only taken my father's life, but was taking mine, as well. He had won.

I tried one more time. "Why do I have to go?" Breaking the silence uncomfortably to my captor, who had become my silent comforter, I was pleading, I knew it, there was no mistaking and I would beg if I thought if I thought it would make even a slight bit of difference. Yet I knew, even as I spoke the words, they were useless; the silent woman looked sombrely at me, as if she was leading me to my death. She was as helpless as I, but was trying hard not to show it.

There was no mistaking the staircase itself. I felt as if I was living my childhood nightmare. In its darkness, I began to climb, holding on to the sides.

The door, which led to the empty dock where I had sat for the last two weeks on trial on my own, opened. Now it was full of guards and there sat Scott in the midst of them.

I couldn't bear to hear the words the judge was using to describe me. Cold. Callous. Manipulative. I sobbed.

Justice was done, according to the crown prosecution service, although when I looked at the prosecution and even at Scott's solicitors, they looked at me like they all felt a great mistake had been made.

I was taken down to the cells to go back to prison. This time, though, it was to begin a life sentence for murder.

The Junior Barrister came down to see me.

"Michelle, the prosecution barrister sends his best. I also heard conversations with Scott and his barrister, his solicitor doesn't want to see him."

"What about an appeal?" I heard myself ask.

"An appeal?" The junior barrister looked confused.

"Yes," I said. "Ken said even if I was found guilty, we would have grounds for an appeal." I had no idea where the words were coming from, my entire mind seemed to have switched off.

"We will be in touch," she reassured me.

"You're suffering from shock, Michelle," she told me. "Life doesn't mean life," she went on to explain. "There will be a recommendation of a minimum term and then you can be released."

It brought little comfort. Scott had won. I now wore the label of convicted murderer. My chance of returning to my community had gone, along with my voice and my rights.

The Junior Barrister handed me a small picture of a woman praying in what seemed like a desolate desert.

"Every time I look at this picture; I can't seem to stop thinking about you." In the midst of the awfulness, it was a gesture of true humanity.

I knew exactly what she meant. The emptiness in which I'd prayed before had just expanded to eternity.

A prison officer had called me the 'lost soul' when I returned to my cell one evening. I was desperate to cling on to something for hope. I drew strength from my prayers. I held on to the picture, still hoping, in spite of everything, that a spiritual force might be with me to face the journey. The journey of not only life in prison, but life for something I had no power or control over. The first night in prison as a lifer would be hard to face.

The woman guard held my hand again to support me onto the van, which was about to take me to face that first night.

"Let them see your face," she said.

The cameras clicked as I walked through the gathered media, holding onto the picture that the Junior Barrister had given me, and a good luck present my now seven-year-old daughter had made for me before the trial.

When I arrived at Newhall, a "listener" was waiting for me in reception. A listener is someone who supports women through times that they may commit suicide. Nothing, prior to that verdict, could have convinced me that a woman who was innocent, could possibly be found guilty.

They processed me, got me through reception by completing the paperwork quickly and I was taken the hospital wing. Over the next few days and nights, a listener sat in my cell with me day in and day out. I told them that I was waiting any minute for someone to admit they had made an awful mistake. I tried to hold onto my faith in God, the higher power, the force of all good that I had found when I was first arrested and sent to Low Newton.

After what seemed an eternity, but was, in fact, the first week of my sentence, I wrote to my mother: I still have hope and faith that I will clear my name. I am writing to my solicitor to start the appeal process he promised in court.

There was hope in the depths of the darkness, and it was pinned on an appeal.

After a couple of weeks, I was placed in the main prison and the other women supported me in the best way they could. Samantha, a young woman in her late twenties, became one of my closest friends at that time. She stood by me every day at work, looking after me. I didn't realise, then, that that kind of shock would continue for years rather than weeks or months. Samantha was coming to the end of a long sentence and had empathy for what I was to face. Life in prison. When I looked at the card on my door to my cell, that was the word under my name; LIFE. Still, I could not link it with me.

Samantha was still a young woman and her life could be started again. She was much like me. She hadn't killed anyone. She had been implicated in other ways. It didn't make sense that she should be sentenced so harshly. She had been at a party when a close family member turned up in need of help because they had killed someone. That person had implicated her there and then and that split second choice she made cost her twelve years of her young life.

Release following a life sentence, she explained, meant serving the minimum tariff and ensuring there was no more risk to the public, by reducing the risk factors which were present at the time when the convicted person *committed* an offence. How could I do that, when I hadn't committed any offence?

"Coward!" I spoke the word out loud to myself often. The word tortured me, knowing the full impact that cowardice had had, not only on my father, but also on my whole family. I had started to internalise the police accusations.

When I spoke to my mum on the phone, she confirmed my thoughts.

"I know you're not guilty," she told me, "You were always a wimp, I should have told the courts how I hit you," her obvious conscience spoke out. Taking a breath, she went on; "But I wouldn't tell them that I hit you when you were holding your daughter. You never once hit me back, or called me a name back, you just stood there like a wimp, crying."

She had no idea that her blunt honesty was cruel and that she had reinforced my worst fears.

I was horrified by my obvious psychological and emotional makeup and how that could possibly be linked to the label of being a lifer, the most dangerous category of prisoner in the prison. With that, it was like I had walked into the gates of Hell in my mind. My conscience for being a coward, the obvious loss and grieving for my father, the inability to assert myself in the world and all the time, having to wear the label of being dangerous.

The lifer manager seemed reluctant to disperse me to the lifer unit in Durham, which was to be my next move. He seemed to know, without saying, that I would not cope with it. Six months after I had been sentenced and with still no response from my solicitors, either on the phone or by letter, I was dreading that move to Durham, without any signs of legal support. "I have to face it sometime," I told the lifer manager. "Better I get it over and done with."

My thinking and my faith in the criminal justice system told me that I wouldn't come back to Newhall after the three and half years I was supposed to spend in Durham, as a first stage lifer unit, anyway. In that time, I would probably have cleared my name.

I left for HMP Durham the very next week. It was the most notorious prison for women at the time. One that holds category A prisoners. A prison within in a prison, I was told.

Durham was as scary on the outside as it was on the inside.

Driving half way into the gate, we stopped and waited for the first gate to close and the second to open. In the gates enclosure, I looked up to the top of the next gate, where a dead crow was hanging.

"This used to be a hanging jail," the officer told me, following my gaze.

The crow was a symbol of recent history. It was 1994 and the last hanging in the United Kingdom was 1964. Thirty years before I arrived there, people were coming to Durham to be hung. The second gates opened to reveal a dusty concrete courtyard, surrounded by hundreds of bleak looking windows facing onto it. Faces peered out of them, so faint that you could hardly see them though the scratched plastic and bars. To the right there was a smaller building with a huge fence around it. This was where the prison housed women, some of whom had committed acts so bad that they were to stay in prison for the rest of their natural lives. I imagined being left here, forgotten by the outside world – my mother, my daughter – people leaving me behind, growing up – giving up the fight alongside me.

Stepping out of the van, once we were secured into the second prison, we approached a small door where a camera peered down on us. Security here was immense. The officer escorting me spoke through the intercom and shortly afterwards, a friendly, grey haired woman with a slight frame opened the door, smiling. I didn't expect such a smile in somewhere so grim and it reassured me, temporarily.

It was not possible to walk through any door inside this prison without the camera and the intercom system. Walking through the door of the wing itself, I began to start to feel a strange energy that I had never felt before. It was a heavy, oppressive energy that I felt, at first, resting on my shoulders and then starting to push down on me, almost like a physical presence. The other women wore a strange look upon their face that I did not recognise at the time – it was one that I would come to know; *institutionalised*. Some of them had remained, for year after year, on this corridor, ironically referred to as a "wing." You had your dinner on this corridor. Association was on it. You worked on it, if you were a wing cleaner. Even slept in your cell that was on it. Everything here was on one corridor. It was the space where you would spend years, only going out for exercise in the dusty yard with helicopter wires above you and windows looking down on you. Whilst you were on this wing, you would be analysed by officers constantly and later, I would learn, *dehumanised*. This place was like living in *Hell*.

"She's on the two's," a male voice bellowed out.

The female officer told me to follow her and I dragged my see-through HMP bags up the narrow metal stairs, which looked like a giant stepladder. I would climb these steps thousands of times before I was to leave this place and would lose three other dear and valuable things to it before I left; my brother, my mind and my dignity.

As I unpacked, many faces came to greet me. There were many insane mothers who had taken their own children's lives. Shunned by the other prisoners, they were desperate to have a friend in the newcomer. I was moved away from them the next day, when another room was made available. That's when Kristie rescued me. A familiar face I knew from Low Newton.

"Michelle!" It felt so strange to hear a familiar voice.

"I'm glad you're here," she grinned, "you can help me with the servery." It was as if she had only seen me yesterday, even though it must have been a year ago.

No one here questioned the fairness of the criminal justice system. It seemed pointless. No one here had a voice that would be heard. The only people who were really able to question the criminal justice system's fairness were those least able to do so – those of us without a voice. The weeks passed very slowly. I tried to take a step back, to see where I fitted into this place. There seemed to be different cultures on different landings. Was it with those who sat on the four's, a cut above the rest? There, they sat and drank tea and coffee all day, generally discussing the behaviour of the others around them, aghast by their crimes, even though they were accused of committing atrocious crimes themselves. I could not fit in with this group.

I also found it difficult to make friends with lifers. Not all, but some, would sit and compare their stories of their killings. It disturbed me and I felt unsafe around them. There were women who had tortured people. I felt sickened by them. I longed for the comfort of my father to make me feel safe, but he was gone. I missed him dreadfully.

A couple of weeks into the incarceration at Durham, I met the probation woman on "the flat." The flat, I was learning the terminology, was the term used to describe the offices, or places on the ground floor. The probation lady, when I first met her, ushered me in and shut the door. She looked nervous.

"I got a message from your probation officer to support you," she explained, smiling. The probation officer she was referring to was the one in Bridlington, who had written a supportive sentence report. She looked at me curiously and lowered her voice into a whisper. "It's a strange prison," she warned, "I shouldn't say this to you, but don't trust anyone, including the officers." I smiled at her reassuringly. I had been given a similar warning by two lifers at Newhall before I left there.

"It's OK, I can do this." These strong words were not a statement for her, they were a statement for me. I no longer wanted to be "looked after."

Kristie, my friend from Low Newton, wasn't to stay long. She wasn't a lifer, or institutionalised like so many of the others. She was merely there because of prison overcrowding issues in 1995.

In the workshop, we worked for £7 a week and made soft toys, ornaments or knitted garments to be sold in shops. The large workshop was split into four sections. The sewing machine area was a small section with four sewing machines – I chose to go there and it would end up becoming my sanctuary.

In the shop adjacent and the farthest room was the knitting section that held all those that couldn't fit in. The main room was the pottery section, where the kiln and the painters worked. The foreign nationals worked happily; many of these women had been muled to bring drugs in. A mule, I would learn, is someone who is used to import class A drugs, who is then reported to the authorities by their importer, to take away the attention from someone carrying in more drugs on the same day. Sentences of eighteen to twenty-five years were the average punishments for them.

The sewing section also attracted foreign nationals. The women happily sewed away on their machines, speaking in different languages. African, Zimbabwe, French.

One of those foreign nationals was to become my closest friend. Mariam, a very elegant and graceful lady, full of dignity and respect for all. She was also wise and warned me, as a friend should, about what was going on in this dangerous environment.

"Don't take the hair conditioner from Lisa," she told me one day, "I have heard them say they are going to put hair remover in it to burn your lovely hair." I was horrified. I could not understand how a human being would want to do this to another.

Thanks, I mouthed, silently.

Having lost touch with my old solicitors, I started to write to new ones to see if there was any chance they would take on my case. There was no legal aid available and I was unable to afford the £600 bill to obtain my summing up from the court, which, I now know, was the place to start for any appeal. I wrote more letters. One to the BBC Rough Justice programme. One to an innocence group. All my case needed was a little scratching below the surface. That had nearly come out in court, in the first trial, but not quite. When the new Criminal Cases Review Commission was launched, I wrote to them straight away. It was, the media told everyone, an independent organisation that would be able to look at miscarriages of justice.

Every night, when I looked into the mirror, I would say the same thing. *Coward*. And every day, I became more depressed and hopeless. I was beginning to realise I was not going to survive this, in spite of my occasional flashes of strength.

On a huge white board, in the office on the second landing, everyone's plan for offending behaviour work was on display for all to see. Katy, for example, was down for an anger management course, substance misuse and a whole range of others. Next to my name lay one course. Assertiveness. I must learn to speak out and defend myself and build up my character. I felt ashamed that everyone could see it, confirming my weakness, displayed there for everyone to see.

The depression worsened.

When we were not working, I wanted to stay in bed. All I could think about was my father and I missed and longed for him. I had started to turn inwards, but in time, that was to become a saving grace. I prayed and meditated every night and sometimes during the afternoon lock up. I decided I wanted to take an inner journey to find myself. For the first time in my life, I focused on developing myself and finding some inner strength. I had lost my father through fear. I was about to embark on the biggest journey of all. To take an inner journey and to face my fears, which had been programmed into my mind since I was only five years old, and battle them.

Chapter 21

"They're like pack animals, like wolves," Tracey told me on the exercise yard one day, explaining the bizarre behaviour of some of the women in Durham. We were sitting on an old wooden bench, identical to the ones you would see in the park, beneath draping trees. Here in 1998, two years from when I first entered the door of HMP Durham, Tracey and I spoke about the negative energy on the wing that we had both felt and that was suppressing us. Everyone could feel it, like an actual physical presence. We discussed a theory that perhaps the energy of those who had been hung here had remained, being reinforced with all the negativity and evil that had come its way since. I imagined how that would be for me; hung for being afraid. Imagine if there were others like me who had been hung, screaming out for justice inside them, like me, with no one to hear their voices.

Tracey was kind – she accepted me as I was. I remained stuck and lost in the longing for my father, but I couldn't speak out because I had been accused of being the cause of that loss. I had been robbed of my right to grieve and try to find comfort. I had, instead, entered an inner world, trying to battle with my nervous and gentle disposition, to gain strength and courage.

People had begun to comment on the peaceful presence they felt in my room – a presence I felt came from my long meditations. Ironically, I was beginning to feel safer in my own cell, away from the intense environment, rather than trapped. It was the most hostile prison I had been in and the women here were jealous of anything, including the attention Tracey was giving me today. She was a high profile prisoner and was breath of fresh air this place. The intense lifers wanted her for themselves.

Many uncaring women had previously watched as my mind had started to play tricks on me following my father's murder. "Play the game," my friend Mariam would advise, as she smiled and spoke to the women who were hostile.

The whole set up was intended to create division. I heard an officer say to another, one day, of their tactics; *divide and conquer* – they had mingled and sat with the women, dividing them through exacerbating the negative talk of other women. Officers would mimic all the prisoners as they walked by them and humiliate them on a daily basis.

"Feeding time for the animals," they would shout and the women had to walk in a single file across and up the landing from the twos and down at the other side like a row of cows, their life meaning nothing, humiliated and ready for slaughter.

Another of my friends was Ronnie, from Low Newton. She, was particularly vulnerable. She was a terrible self-harmer who was serving life for an attack on a friend. I knew when she arrived that she wouldn't cope with the hostility on her fragile mind. I witnessed an officer asking for a fight with her in the workshop. I tried to get her to play the game, as Mariam was teaching me. Two years after her arrival, she committed suicide, her only escape from Durham was through death. No one mourned her loss. She was gone from the criminal justice system, without ever being heard. I will always remember her.

I was going to survive. *Just get through this one day and don't look ahead into the future,* I would say to myself in the mornings. While I was still waiting for a response from solicitors, a woman, Lynn had started to support me. Belonging to the group 'Justice for Women,' she would write to solicitors on my behalf and chase things up for me. I confided to her some of my fears of living on the wing and how it had become a game of psychological warfare. I had chosen the perfect place and time to face my fears; right in the midst of the greatest hostility I had ever experienced.

God help me, I would pray every night and day. I meditated and continued on my spiritual journey, feeling like a spiritual warrior as I faced each new fear, every day. Once I recognised one fear, another one would come up. Until one day, I realised that the two biggest fears of all were losing my mind and a failure to belong that had been instilled by my mother. Both were amplified by the self imposed belief that I was a coward.

I had begun developing psychosis, starting to feel unsafe most of the time. Some of the women had been sectioned and gone to a prison for the insane. That thought scared me to death.

And so, my cell became my spiritual home and I meditated and prayed daily, releasing the negative energy to a higher power.

I was called to the office one morning. I heard the officers talk about me in the morning, before the steel doors were unlocked.

"Get her straight to the office," I heard one of the say. I wondered what they wanted.

When I got to the office, a senior officer closed the door behind me

"Your brother is in hospital," she said, sympathetically. "It's critical; your mother wants you there. We are arranging transport right now."

Neil died twenty-four hours after that conversation. I was by his side when he did. Another Principle Officer supported me to get to the funeral. He was like an angel walking into a dark place. I thanked them both for their support, although the kind PO would have to leave the wing for 'political reasons,' he said.

In the weeks after the funeral, I prayed and meditated more and held onto that as my only saving grace. I could hardly speak now; there were so many things that I couldn't speak about. It had all sent me slightly mad. I felt now as if I had no voice whatsoever.

One evening, I sat on my window ledge, after fully realising how vulnerable I was inside this prison at that moment … and everyone else in it, too. It prompted me to look out and feel a love and compassion for the whole prison and all the lost souls in it. I felt myself rising from the window ledge like I was floating in an empty desert, a void, and suddenly, I was able to face the emptiness inside me. "Don't be afraid," a voice inside me said and I felt a spiritual presence beside me, holding my hand. My heart was able to open up and I felt a pain so huge that it was as if I had taken on the whole of the emotional pain of everyone in the prison. I heard the inner voice again.

I want you to be a voice for prisoners.

Overnight, I was filled with a light and a love so different to the fear and anxiety I had felt. I had released it and in its place was a joy that spiritually, my life had a meaning and a plan and that all this pain and suffering, there might be a reason for it, after all. I might be able to use it to help others. *I was needed. I had a purpose.* I looked into the plastic mirror, stuck to my wall, with the biggest smile on my face. I had a spiritual purpose. I was going to help people from this experience.

I was going to help those without a voice.

The next day, bizarrely, I walked out of my cell the happiest woman alive. I talked freely to everyone like a free spirit that I had become overnight. I couldn't stop the hostility from the officers. Even though I had experienced such a wonder, the negativity, I realised, was still a constant battle on the wing and it remained a daily fight to keep my mind strong. A couple of weeks later, I walked straight into the principles officer's office and shut the door behind me. I had never spoken to him before.

"I need to talk," I told him, boldly. "There might be officers on this wing that might not like us, but I cannot take any more from them." I had been experiencing a high level of hostility from one particular officer and a group of them had become increasingly difficult.

He looked both surprised and confused. I had spoken out!

What have I done, I thought, an hour later, after I had time to calm down. The bullying could now get worse and I have trusted an officer. The fight for survival could get so much more difficult and I was holding on with all I had, for my daughter.

Two days after that conversation, I was put on an early bus and taken to Newhall. The principle officer I had spoken to hadn't told anyone, no one knew anything about me speaking to him. He had just looked into the bullying. I saw him speaking to one of the highest governors seriously, at the end of the wing, following my daring entrance into his office.

"You're going to be OK. I looked into it for you." He said no more. Early the next day, I was being moved with only a couple of hours notice. I had been returned to Newhall, three and half years after I had left, believing I would never return following the outcome of a successful appeal.

Chapter 22

It had been ages since I last wrote to the Criminal Cases Review Commission and pleaded my case. Although it had been so long, I still had hope and faith that that higher power would bring justice for me. Time and again, I would hear the childlike cry- *It's not fair –* echoing in my mind.

One day, it was a Chinese celebration for making promises. "Make a promise," a Chinese lady encouraged me. That's when I closed my eyes and promised I would survive anything. Anything at all and I would never consider a weak way out.

It had all started with a conversation with the education manager, Chris.

"I'd love to do a degree," I told him, "but I'm not good enough."

"You are good enough," he told me firmly. "Of course you are! You can do it."

He wrote a letter to a sponsor to get my first year funded and I started my first year in Social Science on an Open University degree course, questioning social issues and how they changed over time and culture. I started building up my vocabulary with dictionaries; words from the Open University textbooks came to life and my time behind my door studying took me to different places and times, helping me to understand the complexities of the social world.

I was starting to see a future and most of all, making decisions for myself.

My life was now made up of studying in my room, followed by associating with a circle of friends that brought a level of normality to my situation. I started learning survival tactics, such as safety in numbers. The more friends I seemed to have, the less power the few haters had over me. There were three haters, mainly – the same three from Durham. Despite their own heinous crimes, they wanted everyone to know the horrendous crime I was convicted of, to turn people against me. There was nothing I could do. I couldn't speak out and say, *I didn't do it.* I was helpless, but in a different way to the day that my father was killed.

Petty squabbling was always evident on this wing; I meditated every day and chose to ignore comments, but that was definitely so much easier because of my strong circle of friends. People respected me; they would want me to listen to them, or ask for my advice. I flew though my courses, achieving one qualification after another. I went to the gym and my mood and general outlook benefited from the endorphins.

Some women's only safety from the world outside was this prison. They sought comfort and security from each other, huddling together, lost from and confused by the outside world.

Yet this was the same prison which was keeping me prisoner from my family and loved ones. The prison that represented all the lies and the trauma that I had experienced.

The comfort those women brought each other held them together with a sense of purpose and belonging. I loved to listen to their stories. Most of them, I leant, had grown up in a family unit of abuse and had gone on to internalise that abuse. They thought it was their own fault. That they had actually experienced a great crime against them had not been acknowledged, not least by themselves. The system had fooled them into thinking they were worthless. I knew their worth.

I called my daughter regularly, trying to give her as much support as I could as she was growing up. I spent every penny of my canteen on phone cards, going without things the other women would have. Others' bags were filled with jars of coffee and bags of sweets, where mine brought my life line to the only thing I had in the outside world; my daughter. I was her mother and I had to guide and protect her, even though I was in here. A conversation with my daughter lit up my life with a golden light. It was the most important thing in my life, to be able to help her and remain as her mother, guiding her though her life. I sometimes wondered if I would have survived Durham, if I hadn't had my daughter to fight for. If I had not been a teenage mother, perhaps now I would be one of those voices lost and you would not be reading this story.

There were times that we were going through such similar experiences. She was being bullied at school. She had a teacher who didn't like her. At the same time, here I was, an adult experiencing shame and stigma. Who was the prisoner and who was the victim of crime? Surely if the media had got a part of it right, the community would have known her grandfather was killed and she was left without him. Whether her mother was guilty or not, the community shunned a little girl and she often had to cope alone, without support, because of it.

I was paving the way for my release. Health and social care, social science, psychology, anatomy and biology, the knowledge brought my once tired and asleep brain to life. I didn't like TV. I wanted real knowledge of the world we live in. Books, books and more books. I also joined the listeners. I did a training course by the Samaritans. One of them, a lady called Anne, was so compassionate towards me. I was called out, time and time again, to the young offenders wing.

I was asked to help people write letters to solicitors – for this I was called upon many times. Occasionally, a solicitor would visit me here. Again and again, I asked people to scratch the surface of my case. Perhaps go and ask questions of people to find out the truth. No one ever did.

I was to be transferred to Foston Hall. A change in policy meant the prison I was in could no longer house lifers.

Women's prisons are not categorized; they are simply either open or closed. The closed status of Newhall meant that no prisoners were allowed out on day releases, but this was about to change. A new, new semi open wing had been built, which meant some of the prisoners were allowed out on day releases. It also meant that the prison was no longer suitable for closed category prisoners, lifers.

Twenty of us were shipped out within four to five days' notice. The move was a big shock. I had been here now for five years.

Women came to speak to me in the new prison – I knew they were curious because I didn't wear a mask, like the other women. I just tried to be myself.

The senior officer called me over for induction at Foston Hall.

"I just want to use my time and experiences to help other women when I get out of prison." I told her of my ambition to help others.

She smiled at me. "You're just the person that we need. We have a job in the blue room. There's only one thing," she continued. "We have a lady in there with a very strong character, who doesn't like sharing the job."

Early in the morning, I met the security officer outside the blue room. Outside on the steps, there was a large lady smoking a cigarette. She looked on edge, but her demeanour changed to pleasantly surprised and maybe even relieved, when she saw me.

Sharon, as I got to know her, gave me the best bit of advice anyone had ever given me and didn't even realise the power of her words.

"I'm not sure I'm capable of this job," I confided in her. It was a huge responsibility and I wanted to do it properly. The job was to help women resettle into the community, we would find them housing. We would be contacting housing associations and councils on behalf of the women and ensuring their names were placed on waiting lists for their release. Sharon beamed at me with a huge smile. She was a sociopath who didn't normally like people.

"Just get on with it," she said and roared a great laugh.

She was so happy I wasn't threatening or competitive. *Just get on with it* – her words resounded in my mind. I put the fear aside and, as she said, got on with it! I started to organise and plan the work, working through the files carefully. I didn't look at the end of the job – actually getting the women into housing, but just focused on each task and fear started to evaporate from me. Sharon didn't realise she had unlocked a piece of my mind with her straightforward advice. You see, it wasn't even advice for Sharon. She thought my fear was bizarre, seeing an intelligent woman doubt herself.

Before long, the blue room was buzzing with women wanting me to find them accommodation. No fear, I thought to myself, when someone was going out homeless. Just tackle each barrier as it comes up. I contacted local housing associations and got applications sent through the post, completed them and returned them.

"I'm on the waiting list," women would shout, waving a letter triumphantly.

I had grown up independent in one sense, not being able to rely on people, so to have to ask an officer for help was hard. Particularly hard when their eyes glazed over and you knew they didn't have time to do it, or had no intention to do it. They were distracted. Their job wasn't to help, it was to secure. They didn't have time to do both. More often than not, I think, they simply forgot. When a woman asked me to do something, I made a mental note and wrote it down and took it to work. Each time they came up to me and asked if I had done it, I was able to honestly smile kindly and brightly at them in affirmation.

Once, I called a housing association, asking for the latest position on an application I'd sent out.

"Of course," came the reply, "hang on." Then came the question I dreaded. "You're not an inmate are you?"

"Yes," I replied, honestly. "I work in the housing room, helping others with housing. I'm a trusted prisoner."

"I'm not going to speak to you." I passed the phone to my probation officer and smiled sadly at my empowering boss.

"They won't speak to me,"

"Can I ask," she said, after explaining her position as a probation officer, "why you will not speak to a housing worker who is a resident here?" She had a way with words and I was expecting her to take the call for me. She didn't. She passed the phone back to me to continue my job, she was treating me as a human being, based on how I treated her and on what she had seen of me, and not some label.

Chapter 23

In 2005, I was packing my bags again, to be transferred to an open prison for the end of my sentence, but with a lack of hope. Even though I was to be moved to open prison, which meant I was now on my way home, I had nearly served a life sentence. This was the end of a sentence I should not have faced. At the beginning, there was hope. *The truth will prevail;* people had told me. It was something that I had hung onto throughout. God will not forsake me, my spirit told me. My hope had defied all of the oppression, blindly helping me to carry on another day, another week, another month, another season, another year. Here I stood now, at the end of nearly eleven years in prison. It would take me another three years, in open conditions, to prepare for release. My heart sank as I packed to prepare for the end. An end that I should have never had to reach.

My friends and associates wished me farewell and good luck. I knew many of them wished they were in the same position. For me, though, everything had changed. I was able to see my daughter more regularly. I could support her again and be her mother. But it also represented the completion of a sentence for something I had not done. Or done little to prevent. There was a difference, and it was an important one. I was beginning to understand that, in my social setting at that time, there was very little I could do. As an outsider looking in, I had come to understand there were very few people I could turn to. It meant facing people on the outside, whom I had told years ago that I would have had an appeal, because I was innocent. Would they understand the criminal justice and how hard it was to clear my name? Or would they give up and finally think I was guilty? I lost count of the times I told my best friend, Jo, that I had found another solicitor and something was going to be done. Clearing your name after a conviction, however, requires the whole system to admit they were wrong. It is one of the hardest things to do. All my case needed was for one person to gather some information up and work on my case. I wasn't going to give up.

A move like this, to Drake Hall, was a landmark for other lifers. I was glad I was finally on my way home, although, for me, it meant the end of an era of hope that I would clear my name before my sentence had ended. I sat in the bus, hopeless, yet anticipating freedom. It was a strange feeling.

After a couple of days at Drake Hall, I heard my name being called to the resettlement department, where I met Mr Stephenson. He was different to the other officers; he seemed to reveal a little of his personality. My name had preceded me through my probation officer, Karen, who had promised she would ensure I would get a trusted job to help the other women come to the end of their sentence here in Drake Hall, too.

"OK," he said, after listening to what I had done at Foston Hall, "There isn't a place on resettlement at the moment, but as soon as Gill leaves, which will be in the next couple of months, then the job on resettlement is yours."

Gill, I found later, was the most hated woman in that prison at that time and as far as I could see, the hatred was stemming from her job on resettlement.

"I'm not sure if I want it," I told Mr Stephenson. "I'll be quite happy to work on the gardens."

My prison sentence *had* gotten easier during the latter years and I didn't want to be subject to a full prison of hatred at that part of my sentence, like Gill. Working on the gardens was easy. I didn't stand out. I loved being in the fresh air, but sometimes, when thoughts and memories flashed into my mind, I still felt like I was in psychological shock from witnessing my father's killing, feeling helpless and grieving his loss. I soaked up the energy in the fresh air, in the hope that it would heal me. I couldn't reveal that disturbance to any one; if I did, I would be shipped back to closed conditions, on the grounds of not being able to cope.

Eventually, the time arrived that I was to work on resettlement and before too long, I was allowed to go outside to work. I was to travel to Birmingham every day on the train from Stafford, to work for a large organisation. I was to work in a drop-in centre, which helped the local community to find work, training and employment and assisted those who were marginalised, meaning those with a criminal record. I couldn't wait to start. In addition, I would be able to gain skills to pave the way for my dream job. My daughter equipped me with my first mobile phone in 2006. I hadn't a clue how to use it. She spent hours teaching me how to send a text and I learnt to send my first email at work. My daughter was now my teacher.

I texted my daughter on the train at least ten times on the first morning. I had no idea what was and what wasn't acceptable – I was excited! *She hasn't texted me back*, I would think, if she hadn't responded in five minutes.

Are you OK? I would send.

I had absolutely no idea I was being over protective. One day, on home leave, I dropped her off at the university where she studied law. I watched her walk to university, alone.

I've survived for this long, Mum, I'm a big girl now, she would tell me, trying to cope with her over protective mother. She was my baby and nothing had changed for me. I had been stuck in a time warp and at last, I was here to protect her. Only she had grown up.

I had recently tried to get *another* solicitor in the hope of an appeal – I wasn't giving up. The solicitor had said that he would ask a barrister to draft up whether I had grounds for an appeal or not. I opened my letter just after I had picked up my mail at resettlement. My letters were far and few at the end of the sentence. At the beginning, there had been hundreds waiting to be handed out to me. Here, I had to queue and ask if there were any letters. The answer was almost always the same – No! Today, a solicitor's letter was given to me and I had a final hope that my name would finally be cleared before I was released. I opened the letter and there it was in harsh black and white; I skipped to the end paragraph, which read 'No grounds for appeal.'

I couldn't hide my disappointment and shock. The woman sitting beside me was someone that I didn't know that well.

"I have fought my case for years," I told her. "I had this idea that I could overturn my conviction." She smiled, sympathetically.

I put the letter away and changed the conversation quickly.

Just over three years later, I entered the prison gate one day, returning from my out work. I was feeling tense, although that tension wasn't coming from re-entering the institution. Working outside the prison had become a Monday to Friday, routine part of my life and I travelled to Birmingham, supporting people in the criminal justice system. As much as I loved my job, my mind wasn't in it at the moment, I was over-analysing the parole hearing, replaying it over and over in my mind.

The judge had pushed and pushed to see if I would break and admit to a crime that I didn't commit, but I couldn't lie, even if it meant that I didn't have my freedom. Until recently, denying the crime for which you were convicted at a parole hearing meant parole would automatically be denied. Although the law had changed in the last year or so, attitudes had not.

The psychologist knew this and tried to steer the judge towards the new approach. "Even if you kept Michelle for another ten years, she will still say the same thing," That was the prompt for him to push me. He said things about my father, to which I could only reply; "Sorry, that's not true." Not saving my own father had destroyed me.

That hearing was four or five days ago now, and although it was only a short time, it had felt like an eternity, leaving me, once again, in a state of despair. The stress and anxiety was building up to an unbearable level because of what was at stake. A life with my daughter, having my own home, a job.

Walking to my locker at the gatehouse in the prison, my attention was drawn to my left. I had heard a set of jangling keys opening the door separating people in the gatehouse and the staff. Whoever had opened the door was standing now, watching me. I turned to look apprehensively, wondering if something was wrong. At the door stood a female officer, smiling broadly. She was holding an envelope in her hand.

"I've got something for you," she said, her eyes dancing.

I realised, then, that the waiting game was over.

"It's my parole," I gasped. She nodded. "Have I got it?" I asked her apprehensively, without even thinking if I needed to be taken to an office to discuss it. It seemed they were as eager for me to read it as I was. There was no way I could have taken a knock back at this stage of my sentence. It would have killed me. My main aim was to look after my daughter and take care of her; even though she was now a woman, I still ached to protect the small child I had left. My future was sealed in the envelope in the officer's hand. She held it out to me. I froze.

"Open it then!"

"I can't," I replied. "You open it, please."

As she opened the envelope, I watched her reaction carefully. Hope was only a second away and I couldn't bear to see the word '*rejected*' – it would have crushed not only my hope but also every bit of me. I had managed to secure a job for release, so a future was only a moment away ... or not.

She looked at my face seriously, before she cried out, "You've got it!" She threw her arms around me. It was over. The prison part was over. I couldn't believe it. It was only after she released me from her joyful hug that I was able to look at the writing myself, in disbelief.

"I've got it," I said, to no one in particular and looked up at the woman's smiling face. I was struggling to take it in.

"Yes," she shouted, as if the news had turned me deaf. "You've got it." Another lifer was in the gatehouse waiting for her parole. She looked at me with hatred. Walking back with her to the house, I changed the subject, but deep down I wanted to scream out loud. She had wanted hers as much as I wanted mine. I went straight to my room to get my phone card and called my daughter. I told her the good news.

"You've got it," she repeated, just like me. I couldn't wait to see her.

The next day I was called over to resettlement to sign papers and start being processed in the factory of women for release. Just like I had got hundreds of women through resettlement, here I was, myself. I was a person on the resettlement department and not just a face, as the staff had got to know me.

"Congratulations," one of the governors came over to tell me. It was obvious the staff here had respected and valued my input into their team enabling women for release.

A man from the Department for Work and Pensions had come to interview me.

"What are you going to do for money until you start work?" He offered me two weeks' money through the social security department.

"I don't want it," I told him, thinking about the two week gap I had before I started work. The two weeks' money wasn't worth standing in the social security department for. I was going out to a respectable job, supporting people in the criminal justice system, helping them to maintain their accommodation and prevent re-offending. The organisation I worked for gave them temporary accommodation and a support package to enable them in the community. It was everything I had worked for whilst I had been in prison and that hard work was now finally paying off.

I spent the next couple of days packing and giving things away. I was lucky enough not to be going into a hostel; a friend had agreed to give me a temporary release address until I found my own home. I was grateful. It was someone who was a part of a support group who had written and visited over the years and had become a friend. I would want my own place as soon as possible, to be with my daughter, but at least, for now, I had somewhere to go.

My daughter was meeting me at the gates on my day of release.

That morning, I dragged my sacks of belongings to the gatehouse from where I had left daily to go out to work.

"You're not coming back this time," the gate keeper smiled at me. It didn't feel real. Finally, I wouldn't be coming back, but the coming and going from the prison outworking made it feel less of an impact. Perhaps that is what open prison was designed to do; make the impact of transferring into the community less of change. In the time I had spent here, I had got a job and managed to look for places to live. I smiled. I didn't know what to say. I would miss them, but in an obvious way, I wouldn't. The relationship I had built with them was friendly and genuine, but I didn't want to see them again. I felt disloyal, so I said nothing.

"Take care," she called after me as I walked out of the gates. I didn't look back at them, I couldn't. I had learnt much about this day over the fourteen and half years in prison, many had spoken about it.

Whatever you do when you're going home, don't look back at the gates. If you did, it was supposed to mean that you would come back. Gate fever was also something that some women had before release. It was nerves and anxiety that built up, not knowing what they were going out to, no housing, no job, no abusive relationships. My day couldn't come soon enough. I would have been happy in a shed. Nothing and no one would take away my second chance in life.

After all these years, I would finally be able to experience not having anyone to watch me, analyse me, dictate to me, have power over my freedom, be able to analyse me wrongly and affect my life! I just couldn't wait to get away from that gate and not look back.

My daughter and I were reunited at last. I was free on licence and would still be answerable to the criminal justice system, by reporting to probation and letting them know how my life was going. I would also be free to obtain paperwork and speak to people about clearing my name, but I was still labelled as a killer.

It was different, now. I wouldn't explain myself to people if they had thought I was guilty of murder. I would watch the expression of horror on their face as they tried to disguise it. That alone would cause me to feel the horror of the murder again. It would trigger me to re-live the event, knowing how horrific it was and realising that they thought I could actually do that. I said nothing in return, but remained composed, still trying to speak to them in the hope that they might realise, once they got to know me, that I was incapable of such an act. I prayed and still had hope that one day I could clear my name. I would continue to fight, that fight would go on until I took my last breath. I didn't consider that it might take that long. Perhaps the system is designed in a way that innocent people can't fight back.

It's a hard thing to bear that actually, no one really cares, or at least, very few, even though you have experienced a great injustice. Until, like me, you are in it yourself, but at that point it's too late; your voice is meaningless. Your voice has been silenced. You are a criminal. You are nothing.

You are without a voice.

Chapter 24

It was a bank holiday Monday, just after Easter 2013 and I was waiting for Don Cargill to arrive at my house. I paced the living room floor, half apprehensively and half looking forward to what impact passing a lie detector, after years of not being able to have anything solid to prove I was telling the truth, may have on my life.

The wait was giving me a moment to reflect on the last twenty years of my fight for justice, coupled with the painful and torturous grieving process I had put myself through since of the loss of my father *and* the unbearable pain of being accused of that loss. I thought about that impact now, how it had affected my mental health in prison, how it had been escalated because I had not been able to prevent a murder.

It had been five years now, since I was released from prison and although I was still fighting and looking for things that might help to open the doors for an appeal, hope of an appeal was becoming lost. I had accessed counselling from a local general practitioner, for specialist support to cope with post-traumatic stress disorder and she had equipped me with tools on how to cope, now that I was home, even though it didn't feel like I could find a *home* any more. Somewhere I belonged. Counselling wasn't available whilst I was incarcerated and that was a problem that left professionals unable to deal with my response to their questions about the event, when preparing sentence-planning reports. One probation officer wrote,

I find it extremely painful to watch Michelle describe and cope with the intensity of her emotions whilst it is my job to prepare a report, or something to that effect. Another probation officer promised that she would never ask me to speak about the event again, once the report was in. Most professionals that I had spoken with came to the conclusion that I was telling the truth.

Since release, I had been able to try to do things that I hadn't been able to do by myself in prison. I had written and called court transcribers for the summing up of my trial and got a letter back from them saying that court papers had been destroyed, as they only have a five-year retention period. I realised how many unheard miscarriages of justice there might be. I was one of them – someone without a large group campaigning for me on the outside. Someone without a voice. Prisoners who remain isolated and without adequate support, whose papers are disposed of and are therefore lost forever, stand the least chance of ever clearing their names. We only ever hear of the high profile cases that hit the media, momentarily, and even then, they rarely attract as much interest as they did when they hit the media for the crime they were accused of committing. Imagine how many people, like me, whose cases are complicated and therefore harder to prove, being at the scene for instance, are suffering silently behind bars without ever having had any intention at all of committing a crime.

The police interview tapes were also said to be destroyed, although they were a little less sure about their policies than the court transcriber. Over the phone, they said that for serious cases, interview tapes might be kept for much longer, although they did not know how long. The officer's tone was sarcastic. I replied that I knew the charge was serious before, he went on to tell me it had *probably* been destroyed. A letter was sent to me a couple of days after that conversation, outlining the conversation and tidying up that vagueness;

The tapes you requested copies of have been disposed of in line with force policy.

There was an appeal letter enclosed with it, but it was, of course, a fruitless course of action. Whichever was true, I was never going to get sight of them, even if it took my whole life asking for them.

In summary, the whole evidence of there ever being a murder trial in a court was gone. I questioned that process, wondering if it should be a human rights issue and if an organisation might help me fight this. I was left not being able to appeal, on the basis that I had no trial transcript and therefore no summing up. How could I appeal for a fair trial if I had no evidence on record of the one that I had had? How could I argue that it might not have been fair? I called Liberty, the human rights organisation, and was left for days on hold, not getting through. Once again, there was nowhere to channel my voice and no one to support me.

Stigma and social stereotyping had got the better of some of the people closest in my life and in that respect, my life had become unbearable. In fact, living another day had become hard. I had very little support in the community, it was expected that I would get on with my life as if nothing had ever happened. Those closest to me expected me to be able to put it behind me.

For me, taking a lie detector was something I had wanted to do for a long time, but had not had the opportunity. I had asked for this when I was in prison, on remand; however, the solicitor had advised the results of lie detectors were not admissible in an English courtroom. Imagine if it was allowed in the police cells on the day of my arrest twenty years ago, it might have helped the police to understand that, although I was present, I was not a part of the murder. I was way out of my depth as a vulnerable young woman and felt helpless to prevent this horrific crime.

Taking a lie detector now was the only way that I could evidence that I was telling the truth. How I had bizarrely done very little to stop an event from happening; even though I had done little bits, I had not stopped it and, as the police told me, it was clearly not enough. But the truth was, despite all that, I had no intention from the very start and wished no harm on my father. In fact, I had wanted to get him to safety by trying to get him to my house in the afternoon. Just like the barrister said, there was no mens rea, no intention to commit a crime; I was frozen in fear and merely a horrified and helpless observer as a young, vulnerable and isolated woman.

I'd found out about NADAC – the UK's largest polygraph company, and Don Cargill, one if its experts, from a mother of a man who had also been accused of murder at a Yorkshire and Humberside Against Injustice group I had attended in Leeds. She was there fighting to prove her son's innocence and had contacted Don Cargill to help her son. She was determined to clear his name. I struck up a conversation and formed bond with her.

"Your son is so lucky to have you fighting for him," I told her, understanding that fact, because the very small family unit I had come from myself, was not able to give me that kind of support. I broke down and she handed me a telephone number, after I told her my case was hopeless.

I called Don Cargill the very next day and tried to explain my inactive part on the day of the murder, telling him it was not just a case of if I had done the murder, but he must ask questions regarding the plotting and involvement aspects as well. He agreed. The visit was booked only a couple of weeks after that call, on 1st April 2013, a bank holiday Monday. Breaking up for work that weekend, everybody was discussing plans for their long weekend. I had rented a desk space in the office to set up my new charity, *Key Changes*, which aimed to help women combat stigma and give them support with their release from prison.

"I have no plans," I answered, if anyone asked. Deep inside, I knew that if anyone knew what I would be doing that weekend, it would open up old wounds and misperceptions and people would be as horrified as I was about the crime I was accused of. The brutal murder of my own father had to be carried out by someone insane. My story could not be explained in five minutes or even a day. I had learnt better than to disclose what I had been accused of, and the fight against that label, to just anyone. I was at risk of being treated like a social outcast and they had the potential to further damage me psychologically – especially as I still carried the raw pain of torturing myself, as I did, for being a coward.

Regaining a normal life was over for me. My life would and could never be the same. The work I had done, I had excelled at an exceptional rate, as I found myself not being able to fit in socially anymore. It seemed like there was very little left outside the prison for me, weekends away from work were spent alone and isolated, without love, meaning and purpose, similar to those women I was trying to help, who had experienced a life in prison for repeat offending. I didn't want to socialise, as I didn't want to explain the gaps in my life. I didn't want to explain the reason I had never married, or had even had a holiday. For fourteen years, I had studied to gain a career helping women I had become passionate to support. To help those women in prisons with whom I had served time alongside, who were often misunderstood and the majority of them had been victims of serious crimes themselves. Their lives had then got out of hand and they turned to things like drugs and alcohol to blot out the mental damage that had been caused. They then got into the vicious circle of offending and they found, like me, that there were no second chances for them in the outside world. I wanted to help them.

Today could mark a new start, I thought, for the rest of my life. For the first time in twenty years, I began to feel a new kind of hope. At last, I would be able to prove to my loved ones and new friends that, although I was present at a murder scene, I was a horrified observer. They might then try to understand a small part of what might have gone on in my mind, as part of that horror, to disable me in the way that it had and how that horror and helplessness might have impacted upon me.

Knowing I was going to take the lie detector test had made me relive the whole incident the night before. That was when my mind reminded me that I didn't do anything wrong, but, in that lonely place, my mind tormented me, telling me I had been a coward and a pathetic character. That character had cost my father his life and my daughter a mother. All those years of my mind tormenting me came back to me with a vengeance.

My journey of being accused of something I had not done was a journey I would wish no one else to take. I know there is no way that some people would possibly understand that situation; I thank god for their ignorance. Ignorance really is bliss. However, ignorance in the legal system is dangerous. Very dangerous. It makes hundreds of people, like me, suffer a lifetime of horror, having people trust the criminal justice system and not question it, because they do not believe something like this could ever happen to them. I wish I did not know about how people are forced through a black and white criminal justice system as human beings with complex emotions and relationship dynamics. I would not wish what I went through on my worst enemy. It is torture to go from someone whom is viewed as good, gentle, kind and giving, to a manipulative murderer overnight.

I relived the police interviews now, as I waited for Don and the stark truth and awful truth of being led into a trap of looking guilty of a murder was, I am sure, hard for anyone to believe.

When I answered the door, Don Cargill walked into the living room. I knew immediately, from his very presence, he was a man marked with integrity. He was honest and didn't suffer fools lightly. He was here for truth and that was all. He was a truth seeker; his career marked him well for that. "Tell me the story," he said, sitting on my sofa.

"It's a long and unbelievable story I told him," praying that he would understand how gullible and stupid I had been.

"Try me," he invited, strength of character radiating from him.

I explained the shock and the horror and the unbelievable story of being carried miles away to a remote place and how I had done nothing. How the psychological distress, shock and disbelief had immobilised me. The first time my brain came out of shock was when Scott was pouring the petrol over my father. And then, all I said, I explained, was 'what are you doing?'

Don nodded his head, taking it all in. We formulated the questions together to ensure they covered everything. The plotting and an understanding of how big the psychological impact might have on my brain to function normally.

Attaching me to the lie detector in my living room was scary. "Just relax," he said.

"Were you the one who killed your father," Don asked firmly and clearly.

"No."

"Did you ever discuss, plan with, ask or in any way persuade Scott to kill your father?"

"No."

"Was the first time you realised Scott was going to kill your father was when he set fire to him?"

"Yes."

He looked at the results on the sophisticated equipment he had set up on the table in my living room. He gave nothing away, his expression unreadable. This was a strong man, clearly looking for the truth and would take no prisoners if there were any flaws.

As he came to take off the wires from my hands, he looked me straight in the eyes.

"What do you think the result is?"

"I've passed," I told him, finally relieved that I could go on with my life with a little bit of dignity.

"With flying colours," he beamed.

Now all I had to do was to prove to the world that I did not kill my father. I had to clear my name, despite all the legal barriers.

Lightning Source UK Ltd.
Milton Keynes UK
UKOW05f2128230417
299711UK00007B/78/P